AYO ISOLA

# Succeeding in Business

Practical approach to Solving Business Puzzles

# SUCCEEDIN G IN BUSINESS

*Practical Approach to Solving Business Puzzle*

Ayo Isola

Succeeding in Business



***Published and Package by***
Kronikus Global Publishers
+234 810 305 3201
Micholak19@gmail.com

ISBN: 978-978-908-985-7

For all information address all correspondence to the author www.ayoisola.com

Printed in the Federal Republic of Nigeria

## *CONTENTS*

## *Dedication*

To God Almighty Himself who is the most successful business guru that ever lives.

To every start-up trying to find its path in the business world, you can do it and successfully get there.

## *Foreword*

In the ever-evolving landscape of business, where challenges and opportunities intertwine, navigating the intricate pathways to business success demands a combination of insight, resilience, and strategic acumen. As we embark on the journey laid out within the pages of this book, it is my pleasure to introduce a guide that transcends conventional wisdom and offers a fresh perspective on the dynamics of achievement in the entrepreneurship world.

This book is not just a manual; it is a compass, expertly crafted to guide aspiring entrepreneurs, seasoned business executives, and anyone with a passion for success through the multifaceted terrain of the business realm. Written by Ayo Isola, a seasoned entrepreneur with a wealth of experience, "Succeeding in Business" is a testament to his dedication to unraveling the intricacies of triumph in the competitive and dynamic world of entrepreneurship.

Throughout these pages, you will find a rich tapestry of insights, case studies, and practical strategies that goes beyond the theoretical, offering a pragmatic approach to overcoming obstacles and seizing opportunities. It is a thoughtful exploration of the fundamental principles that underpin success in the business arena, combined with real-world examples that illustrate the application of these principles in diverse contexts.

The author's commitment to empowering readers with the knowledge and skills needed to thrive in today's fast-paced business environment is evident. From cultivating a resilient mindset to embracing innovation and fostering effective leadership, "Succeeding in Business" equips its readers with a holistic toolkit for not only surviving but flourishing in the face of uncertainty and change.

As you delve into the chapters that follow, may you find inspiration, actionable insights, and a roadmap that propels you toward your goals. "Succeeding in Business" is not merely a book; it is a companion on your journey to excellence, offering guidance and wisdom to help you navigate the challenges, capitalize on the opportunities, and ultimately carve out your own path to success.

I commend Ayo Isola for this insightful contribution to the literature of business success. May the wisdom contained within these pages serve as a beacon for those who seek not only financial prosperity but also fulfillment and significance in their entrepreneurial endeavors.

***Peter Akinbowale (SPA)***

# Introduction

Only business can make you wealthy. If you plan to be an employee, you cannot live your desired life; working for other people will rather make them rich while putting you into perpetual financial slavery. Though, starting a business in a country like Nigeria can be very tiring, but then, it makes you strong and develop in you this tenacity toward success. Hence, owning a business in Nigeria is not for the faint-hearted, only strong people can start one and sustain its viability, though, every country's challenges are peculiar. Businesses in Nigeria will thrive more if there are people who would simply have the mind and strong heart for entrepreneurship.

Almost every month, many businesses shut down and liquidate, not because they feel like quitting, but because some of these businesses are faced with severe economic difficulties. Success in business can only be determined by how well and how far the business owner can see - many businesses start without the end in picture.

There are several principles that will make a business to succeed, if they are toyed with, defeat is inevitable. One of the principles of achieving and sustaining a great success in business is a working vision. Vision is the ability to see the future the way it could be, which means if you cannot see the future of your business the way it could be, then that business may not see the light of the day. This is one of the big mistakes business starters make, they don't see the future, not to talk of knowing what will take them through to the future of their business.

Many successful entrepreneurs and businesses today succeed not because they started their business with a huge capital, most of them started from absolutely nothing, some started with a very low capital, but one thing is, they started with a very good vision.

Though, aside from the vision you would have when starting a business, there are other factors that will also act as a catalyst to the success of your business. Starting a business requires reviewing, making decisions, conducting market research, and gaining expertise in areas you never imagined. The process of starting a company requires considerable time, effort, and resources, from the initial idea phase to the final launch. While certain aspects of the process may be unique to your particular business, there are many similarities that most entrepreneurs encounter as they begin their ventures. In this guide, we've broken down the initial steps you'd want to take when starting your own business.

Anybody can make a good and successful business owner, but not everybody can make a good and successful business owner. The capacity to make a successful business owner out of you lies solely on your ability to have a determined mind, strong will, and the drive to make it in whatever business you want to build.

Typically, there are three sets of people in business: those who want to build a business empire, those who want to build a street business, and those who just want to survive as a business owner. Well, don't aspire to be a person who just want to survive in business, rather be someone who wants to build a business empire.

All things are possible and it all will start from your mind and the vision you have for the business you are starting or doing. It is quite unfortunate that lots of people do business for the wrong reason these days, unlike the days of Henry Ford, a man who built a business empire for himself, and not even for himself alone, but for his generation and generations to come. A man who had a vision that Ford as a company could build beautiful and luxurious cars. Today, we have Ford motors as one of the best gifts to the human race.

We also have the example of Aliko Dangote, the richest man in Nigeria, if not in the whole of Africa as at when this book was written, who started his company with just a little amount of money, but saw a great vision for his business and thereby built an empire for himself. In one of his interviews, Aliko Dangote said he wanted to build a business, creating products for everyone and for every household, that it would come to a time when every household wouldn't be able to live or do without his products on a daily basis.

This is true today; Dangote Group has grown and spread wider than every other business in Africa. I can imagine the number of people buying Dangote products each day. You would buy Dangote cement if you must build a house or probably do some constructions. If you don't buy the cement, you will buy foodstuffs, unless you want to go hungry, and so on. Right now, Aliko Dangote just launched his refinery some months ago. This refinery, as a matter fact, is the largest oil refinery in the world as at when this book was written. So typically, there is no one who would do without Dangote's products each day or moment.

Aliko once said, "To be successful in business, you must be focused, hardworking, and passionate about the business you are doing." Dangote's impact expands beyond his business, he is a man who has grown to be a philanthropist with his aim of empowering the African nations.

The two successful businessmen I have mentioned earlier are people who are focused and vision-driven, who are not only motivated by the incentives or what they will get from business. Rather, they are motivated by the great impact they want to make, by the value they want to push out to the world and also the later generations. In the same vein, you must be motivated by what you want to offer, the impact you want to make, and also have the future generations in mind in order to be a successful business owner.

Success in business is possible, but the term 'success' as it is, is not a generic term, it is rather a personal phenomenon. Which means, what success is, is quite different from person to person. To one, success might mean to make more impact and affect more lives positively with what they are offering. To another, it might mean accruing or generating more income into the company's account, yet to somebody else, success might mean building a global business empire that affects every sector you can ever mention.

Whatever it is that you want to achieve in business, just have it in your mind that one of the things that will make you a success is to know exactly where you are starting from, where you are, and where you are heading to. This is one of the essences of this book! *Succeeding in Business* is a book I deliberately wrote to inform you about the right mindset and approaches you should have for business, that regardless of who you are, your age, status, race and color, you can always make it, and to drive your mind towards achieving a great success in business.

You see, just know this right, that if people like Jack Ma, the co-founder of Alibaba group, can make a big deal out of business, then you can also make a big deal out of your business. If he could start from nothing and amount to something in his business, then trust me, you can also build something great out of your nothing.

As you read this book, you will see me pour out my heart as I'll be sharing deep thoughts and secrets that will make you an astounding business owner. Whether you are a newbie or a long-term business owner, whether you are currently failing in your business or not, whether you are doing well or not, just understand the simple truth that you can always do better than what you are doing at the moment.

If you have laid hands on this book and are presently reading, I so much congratulate you because this will be a great revelation for you. It will give you reasons to be more driven and focused than ever before, help you to develop a strong vision and make a difference in your business endeavors.

I know you want to be successful and that's why you laid your hands on this book in the first place. If this is true, get ready to walk with me on this journey of success in business!

## Chapter 1

# The Right Mindset

***The key to success in business is to focus our mind on things we desire not things we fear***

-Brian Tracy-

I started building my business world many years ago when I was in high school. I remember selling graph books to some of my classmates in the class. I discovered that I had the passion and mind for business, and that is one thing about business. It's either you have passion for what you want to do or you develop an idea. From the beginning of my life, I already had the business mindset; as I was growing older, I developed the mindset that I would be doing business so I can impact my generation and those to come. During those times, I already had the mandate of God upon my life, so I signed up to the fact that I would be doing business and would also be in ministry.

Mindset is everything. By God's grace, since the inception of my life till now, I have not applied for any public or civil service role. I have always wanted to do business, because I'm also aware that one of the ways to make great impact is to invest in business.

In *Success is Who You Are* - one of the most powerful books written by Dr. Sam Adeyemi many years ago, he made it known that for you to be successful, you must have a full conviction about yourself that you are already a success, because the way you see yourself is what you would look like in the nearest future. Literally, you can never attract what you are not. I will explain better.

The truth is that for you to be successful in any of your endeavors in life, you must first attain that same level of success within you before it will come from your outside environment. Your thinking capacity must be hyperactive and positive when it comes to achieving success. If you cannot see yourself as a successful person from within, you should not expect success outside of you.

What I am saying is that, if you must be a successful business owner, you must go all the way to think of success from within. The success you cannot see or attain from within, you won't attract from outside.

Most businesses died in a few months of the start! This is quite unfortunate because most start-up owners do think all they need to start and run a successful business is money. Some would go as far as saying they need thousands or millions of dollars before they could start a business, but this is not true. When it comes to the success of a business, what you need first is not money. Many failed because they thought they needed a lot of money to start out. Well, you may be disappointed to find out that all you need to survive as a start-up owner is not money, it is rather your thinking faculty. It is one thing to have a nice business concept, it is another thing to have the right mindset towards the business. Which means, if you do not have the right mindset, you cannot survive or succeed as a business owner? Developing a positive mindset will allow you to have the right business idea.

## Developing the Right Business Idea

As earlier stated, if you must succeed as a business owner, you must develop the right business idea. The starting point to success in business arises from your idea development. It is idea that rules the world, not necessarily money, though I've heard a lot of people say money rules the world. Well, I can argue that this is not true, because you must generate an idea before you will generate an income. Without idea creation, there can't be wealth creation.

Generating business ideas is the first and one of the most important steps for any entrepreneur. Lack of a good one will make it tough to get your business off the ground. Allow your mind to thoroughly work first if you are aspiring to start a new business, and discern on which idea to settle for, because you should not simply show up in the business world all because your friend is also successful in a particular business path. Always remember that what works for your friend may not work for you.

The following will help your business idea generation:

- *Brainstorm on various ideas.* The first step in selecting the business idea is determining the appropriate type of business. Finding a business idea is as important as finding a hobby you are okay with, your personal objectives, and your abilities. These, among many, are critical steps you should consider, so that you can be motivated and increase your chances of success.

After brainstorming on a few business ideas, especially those you're passionate about, then comes the research stage. The research stage is when different types of ideas are looked into and an understanding of how much work each one will require is developed. After much scrutiny and you have gotten a final list of ideas that have not been crossed out, you should validate them in the market just to determine if they will be profitable and successful.

- *Make a business plan.* Building a business plan is necessary for you when starting a new business. Before investing a significant amount of money and effort into your business idea, there is a need to analyze your concept and develop a good plan. A business plan will compel individuals to simplify their ideas into a clear image of what they intend to sell, why they intend to sell it, and how they intend to sell it. As a business owner, you need to understand that creating a business strategy involves considering the time and resources required to get your business concept started. Weigh both the pros and cons of your business idea and develop a strategic business plan to make it a success.

- *Analyze market demand*. Before you start a business, you need to research your target market and the optimum customers for your product or service. Consider how your business can uniquely solve your customers' problem. This is necessary, because it is not enough for you to start a business, what's important to you is problem solving and value giving. If your business is not focusing on what products or services your customers would want, then the idea may not see the light of the day.

Consider what they would do in the absence of your product or service. This would also be an excellent time to undertake competitive research and see why consumers or customers are gravitating towards a particular company and figure out what you can do better to overtake and be better than them. Additionally, determine whether your business concept has sufficient demand to be viable, because it can be challenging to enter a market if there is more competition than demand.

- *Test your business idea.* Successful business owners test their ideas. If your business must thrive and succeed, regardless of your experience level, you should test your business idea before allocating the time and money necessary to implement it. This will give you an adequate understanding of whether you are truly prepared to execute your business idea and embark on the journey of a new business adventure. There are numerous ways to accomplish this, but one common and easy way to get it done is by having a one-on-one engagement with an entrepreneur who has previously worked in a similar sector. You can discuss every facet of the business and attempt to understand everything there is to know about it, and if the person is willing to share wisdom and knowledge with you, then it will be a great advantage to your start-up journey.

While speaking with the entrepreneur, you can ascertain whether you are prepared to take on the mentioned tasks. You should then begin to work on your business establishment only if you are confident and have tested the business idea in the real world.

- *Consider profitability*. I must say at this juncture that the main aim and objective of every business owner is to make profit, no business owner wants to continue running his business on loss and lack of customers. So, when selecting a business idea, the final factor to check is its profitability.

The profitability of any product or service is determined by several criteria, including its necessity, market size, marketing costs, manufacturing costs, retail value, and scale of production.

Your business idea may appear excellent and sound great and good in every way, however it will be a fruitless endeavor if it cannot generate profit for you. This is why entrepreneurs should take the time to properly comprehend and protect their business's earning potential before starting out their venture.

## Creating Your Business

Once you've got an idea and know that there's a demand for it, you can get started on making it a reality. Below are some standard starting points in getting a business up and running.

- *Be flexible.* It's important to remember that business ideas are rarely perfect from the get-go. Be open to adjusting your plan, budget, and ideas as the needs arise. Try to avoid major last-minute changes, however, because they can have effects down the line.

You need to be willing to learn more also; business isn't successful because it has a great plan and viability to break through. Business becomes a great success because the entrepreneur is open, willing, and flexible enough to learn, relearn, and unlearn new strategies that could make the business a great success.

- *Research the market.* Whatever the idea you may have, your product or service will be aimed at a specific group of people and/or at meeting specific needs. It is then a requirement to research the market you plan to serve. The results of that research will be the foundation of your customer service philosophy. Decide how you're going to serve your customers, through what channels, and what is easier or more accessible for your client base.

  Most business owners made this mistake when they started their new business; they understood their business ideas, what it takes to start a new business, but not their market structures. If you fail to understand your market structure before you start any worthwhile business, you may fail because the market may not be favorable to you.

  Market research is important to get an accurate read on the real problems, hardships, or difficulties your prospective customers face. There are different challenges that face customers/consumers, and it is your thorough research that will give you an accurate insight about how to deal with the situation and also get you ahead in your business endeavor.

- *Set deadlines.* Lastly, set a deadline to kick-start your business. This can be a useful tool to help keep your goals on track. With firm deadlines, you can help yourself maintain boundaries, recognize what is plausible and implausible for you, set detail-oriented goals, and measure your success.

  Setting a deadline and being keen on your deadline will enable you to do away with procrastination. As a business owner, procrastination should not in any way be in your dictionary or you will jeopardize the chance of your success in business.

## What Makes a Great Business Idea?

A successful business idea addresses a real market need, offers a unique value proposition, and has the potential for scalability and profitability. It should be practical and achievable with available resources, and adaptable to market changes.

As we will see, small business ideas are just the first step in a long line of considerations for developing a successful business. To get there, you'll need to evaluate not just your idea potential, but also your potential to see it through.

## Mindset is Everything

To cap it all, your mindset as a business owner is as important as protecting your name as an individual. If you cannot keep a healthy mindset, you won't be able to keep a healthy business, because to be a very successful business person, you must be aware that your mind can shift or stagnate your business. On a daily basis, you must see that your business is moving forward, not backward. Be ready to see opportunities in every problem.

The way you think and see things matters a lot. Your thoughts, if you are having the right ones, will enable you to uncover and see problems as opportunities, and then turning those opportunities into something profitable for your business. It is an understanding that everything around us is a result of someone having an idea and then executing it.

## Believe in Yourself and Your Business

You have to be resilient and be able to continue building what you believe is the next best thing. Things you build will often not succeed, but ultimately, those losses will add up to a win, based on what you've learned and believed.

Things would always go wrong, problems will always come, but you need to have a resilient spirit, this will help you bounce back from any down moment.

So, ultimately, don't just ask yourself, "What is happening right now?", this may not be the right question to ask in a challenging time, but a question like "What will happen three steps forward or away from the action I'm going to take today?" will allow a free flow of answers to your mind.

## Think Big and Act Accordingly

A business owner must be a great thinker if he must succeed in his business! Your mental faculties, if working well, will make you think about innovations instead of shallow thoughts. Now, the question I want you to answer right now is do you want to make a big deal out of your business? Then, you must learn to think big and act accordingly. Know that it is not enough for you to think right or big, it is also important to act in the direction of your thoughts.

You have to think and take precept-by-precept steps. Your thinking must go in the same direction with your day-to-day decision, be articulate, and also believe in yourself that you can make it in the business sector. Practically, you need to have the mindset that your business will grow and thrive. This mentality will enable you to have the big picture of the future of your business on your mind. Why? In the end, what you believe is what you eventually become. Therefore, look at the big picture and give direction to the overall vision. This is the business mindset that will lead you to success.

## The Growth Mindset

As a business owner, you must have the heart for growth! Settling for less shouldn't be in your agenda. If you are aiming for growth, also have a positive disposition towards it. Many businesses don't survive because their growth capacity is not on a high side. If you believe somehow that you're set to a certain capability and level of accomplishment, you'll never achieve anything more.

However, if you believe you can get better and do things better, then your growth mindset will enable you to accomplish more.

You need to have the mentality that you can teach yourself to do anything if you push yourself hard enough and try things out for yourself. If you must grow, you must also study. It takes a great deal of discipline and conscious learning for a student to graduate from one level to the other. Without conscious learning and study, a learner will rather remain stagnant and not move forward. This is also true for businesses. For yours to experience growth and expansion, be willing to stretch yourself, your mental capacity and do more; which means, you will be willing to attend business seminars, buy courses, and also upgrade the scope of your business, because it is learning that breeds upgrade and upgrade breeds growth.

## Chapter 2

# Businesses You Can Do

*Successful entrepreneurs know that the best way to predict the future is to create it*

-Peter Drunker-

There are thousands upon thousands of businesses anyone can do out there. Only a frivolous individual will give an excuse that there are no businesses out there. On a daily basis, people are quitting their nine to five jobs to start their own businesses. If anyone can do a business, you can also do one; you can go into business and be a great success in it.

In this chapter, I'll be sharing with you those business opportunities you do see around you on a daily basis. One of the reasons most people are broke and refuse to start a business is because they are always seeing problems and challenges, instead of seeing and seeking ways to proffer solutions to the problems they see. Not many know how to turn a problem into an opportunity. This is a great challenge, as it is a problem not to identify problems as opportunities. You need to understand that unto every problem there is an opportunity therein, you just have to open your mind wide and try to give answers to every question in your mind.

If you are used to the common phrase 'there are no businesses again', you need to erase it from your mind, now. This, among many other challenges, is what diverse people face everywhere in the world, not only in African countries alone.

Most love to do business, but don't know which one to do. These sets of people are the most confused beings you will ever meet in your life. They turn out predominantly to be multi-talented, gifted in doing so many things at a go. They have many ideas, but they don't know which of them to choose.

There are those who have great business ideas, but don't know how to start out or where to start from. Meanwhile, there are still others who are expecting millions of dollars to start their businesses. Great business owners you see out there are people who started their business from nothing, only with their vision and little money they had on them. They are open-minded people who believe in innovation and that they can make it, so they ventured out.

As earlier stated in the previous chapter, the first step to take when starting a new business is to generate ideas. Many aspiring entrepreneurs dream of starting a business, but finding a viable idea can be challenging. In the digital age, selling products and services online presents a vast array of unique, affordable start-up options. The key is to match your interests, strengths, and skills to an online business idea that can help fill a need in the market and grow into a profitable endeavor.

Very briefly, I will be sharing with you some businesses you can start with very little capital. Before I share these ideas, I want you to understand that the world is now going digital, because of course, we are in a digital world. Therefore, with hundreds of business ideas, you can start wherever you are and with whatever you have at your disposal.

With hard work and diligent planning, you could soon own and maintain your business, market it digitally, and also has the freedom to be successful anywhere in the world.

## Businesses You Can Do

I just want to share my vast knowledge with you as an individual who is also experienced in the business world. I also believe that if I can successfully run a business, you also can. If I can start my business from nothing and grow it into something, then I believe you can also plant your business idea and make it into big enterprise.

With the little amount of money, you have on you, there are hundreds of businesses you can do, especially when you find yourself in a country like Nigeria, you have great advantages unlike many other European countries where you can't just start a business without some legal backing.

Where we have over 200 million people in Nigeria, your business will thrive if only you would start from somewhere and grow thereafter. However, some business ideas I want to share with you can be done anywhere in the world given that you're ready to put in your efforts and make things better for yourself.

Here are some of the businesses you can do anywhere in the world:

- ***Farming:*** Talking about Nigeria as a country, the agricultural sector is contributing about over 20% to the overall GDP of the country, even though it can be much more. The sector is one of the most flourishing sectors of the Nigerian economy. With proper and strategic planning, anyone with basic knowledge of farming and manufacturing operations can start a profitable agriculture business.

  You don't need a huge capital or farmland to enter the agriculture business. If you have a little piece of land at your backyard, you can still plant some crops in small or vertical containers to get the most out of your space.

  Farmers are really making a lot in farming business, so it is a business you can do. Start with whatever you have on you, learn all you can and launch out. Agriculture is a very essential and important part of everyone's life, no one can survive without using a farm product for days. If you love to farm, I will strongly encourage you to turn your passion into a business. Farming is one of the widely used ones as a successful business idea.

- ***Rental Services:*** One of the numerous business opportunities around you as a Nigerian is rental services. The rental services industry is a broad one in the country, encompassing car rentals, event rentals (such as canopies and chairs), and even house rentals. The demand for rental services is high, especially in major towns where events take place regularly.

  Starting a rental services business requires strategic planning. If you focus on renting out canopies, tables, and chairs, you can cater to the needs of individuals and organizations hosting events. Choose a suitable location and establish a strong network to ensure a steady stream of customers.

- ***Catering Service:*** Do you love to cook and you can cook? Have people ever applauded you for one or two delicious meals you prepared for them? Then start cooking! Launching a catering business may be the perfect small scale business idea for you. You can cook at home and deliver to various parts of your city. There are catering vendors who cook in the comfort of their two-bedroom apartment and get their food delivered via riders.

Everyone has to eat, no matter who they are or where they live. And depending on what works for you, you can set it up as a physical restaurant or an online food delivery business. All that matters is for you to create something that resonates with your target market and budget. For example, you could set up an online food delivery business targeting areas with offices and workplaces since many workers would rather order in than leave their office for lunch, or you could consider a physical space if your target market is in a rural location or if your customers don't have experience with online food delivery platforms.

Of course, quality is essential if you're selling food. I strongly recommend brushing up on your cooking skills if you're starting this venture alone. You can also partner with a more experienced cook if you need culinary skills.

- ***Property/Real Estate Investment:*** Have you ever thought of investing in a real estate? If not, why not consider it? Real estate investment takes more upfront capital than some other small business ideas in Nigeria, but if you have the capital, you should definitely look into purchasing land(s) or property(ies) in Lagos. The returns can be as much as 100% - 200% profit when you resell them. You may presently have a big or spare apartment that your family is not occupying, you can lease them out, and you will earn your money. You can also partition your unused apartment to an office space and then lease it out to those who are in need of it. With this, you will make a reasonable passive income either on a monthly basis or annually.

- ***Day Care Center:*** Nigeria's demand for reliable day care centers presents a unique business opportunity. Many of these centers don't meet the high standards that parents expect. This gap in quality child-care services creates a promising avenue for entrepreneurs. You can easily start this if you have the creativity, love for children, and access to a clean and secure environment.

  Embarking on this venture doesn't necessitate intricate skills or elaborate setups. What matters is your passion for providing a safe and enriching space for children to learn and play. This business idea's foundation lies in understanding parents' specific needs and concerns. Plan smart, keep kids safe, teach creatively, and create a day care that parents love and where kids thrive, bringing you joy.

- ***Sports-viewing Center Business:*** I told you earlier that there are several businesses you can do. Don't undermine any idea, just give it a chance. People are dying of hunger and poverty all because they have no money to sustain themselves, but laying your hands on some businesses can make you realize that there are other big businesses you can venture into, but you must just start from somewhere.

  Sports-viewing centers have become a popular business opportunity in Nigeria. Many individuals in villages, towns, and cities do not have direct access to sports channels and rely on viewing centers to watch their favorite games. To start one, you will need a suitable site, a well-equipped structure, comfortable seating, and the necessary gadgets for showing games. Over time, you can build a loyal customer base and create a thriving business.

- ***Make-up Business:*** Do you have love and passion for beauty? You love it more when people look beautiful and attractive? Does it get to you when you see rough or bad make-up on people's face? Then, why not consider going into a make-up business?

  The beauty industry has evolved significantly, with make-up becoming more than just a beauty item. There is nowhere in the world where ladies or women don't wear makeup; at least 60 to 70% of ladies do, which means, it will be a viable business for you if you engage in it. The business is now considered a form of creative art and an essential component for various professionals such as models, artists, photographers, and actors. Starting this business will allow you to provide make-up services for special occasions like weddings and birthday events. Additionally, you can offer training classes to generate extra income. With the right skills and the passion for beauty, you can turn your love for make-up into a successful business venture.

- ***Laundry Services:*** There are people who are too busy to wash and iron their clothes. This alone makes the laundry business very profitable and viable. The business is a profitable small-scale business that requires minimal technical skills. In a fast-paced society, many people have little time to spare for laundry, making laundry services in high demand.

To start a laundry service, find a favorable location in a busy area, especially near offices where there are professionals. Start with a small team and gradually expand as your customer base grows. Providing quality service and timely delivery will help you build a loyal clientele.

- ***POS Business:*** I am not aware of how viable the POS business is or will be in other countries, but in a country like Nigeria, it is a very lucrative venture. The Point of Sale (POS) business provides a fast and convenient alternative to traditional banking. Instead of queuing for hours at the bank or ATM, people can now conduct basic financial transactions at a POS machine, saving them time and effort.

  Embarking on this venture involves setting up stands or shops in strategic locations. By offering quick withdrawals and other financial services, you can attract customers and earn a fee on each transaction. Establishing a chain of POS stands across different areas can further expand your business and increase profitability.

POS business is one of those many businesses that most young champs are doing today. If you don't have any business at the moment, consider doing it. It is better than sitting in an armchair all the time with nothing tangible to get busy with.

- ***Hairdressing Business:*** Hairdressing is an evergreen small scale business opportunity. People always strive to keep their hair in the best shape possible, keeping hairdressing services in high demand.

  To open a hairdressing salon, you need to be a professional hairstylist or employ skilled hairstylists. Offering quality services and recommending hair care products to clients can help you build a loyal customer base.

Additionally, you can train apprentices and sell hair products for additional income.

- ***Barbing Services:*** Barbing, like hairdressing, is another thriving small-scale business. Men need regular haircuts and grooming services, making a barbing salon a necessity in every neighborhood. To start a barbing salon, you need to acquire the necessary skills or hire skilled barbers. Providing quality services, selling grooming products, and offering training can help your barbing salon stand out and attract a loyal clientele.

- ***Road Transport Business:*** The road transport sector in Nigeria is a thriving industry, with millions of people relying on road transportation for their daily activities. Starting a road transport business allows you to cater to the transportation needs of individuals and businesses.

The scope of your road transport business can vary depending on your capital level. You can choose to focus on intra-state movement within a city or expand to inter-state transportation. Providing safe and reliable transportation services and building a strong network of drivers and vehicles will contribute to the success of your business.

- ***Bookstore:*** Starting a bookstore is another excellent business in Nigeria. There are several bookstores that started from the scratch and later rose to the level of employing more workers to work for them. All you need is to get a great space and fill it with books. These books can be anything from faith or spiritual to motivational books and other related items. Just study your environment, think about what people need, think about the kind of books they may probably admire and give it to them.

Also, your bookstore doesn't have to deal only in new items. You could sell used books at cheap rates and move merchandise quicker. Regardless of what you choose to sell, your bookstore will thrive and make you more money if it's in a great location and your books are of good quality.

In fact, there are vendors selling hardcopy books on a digital platform. Just snap and post the book you wish to sell on your social media space, put the price tag and sell.

- ***Car Wash Business:*** Car wash business is among the businesses that are also thriving in Nigeria. Car wash companies are quiet but significant money makers. Think about it: many car owners visit a car wash, even if it's just twice in a month. Considering there are over 20 million cars on Nigerian roads, that's a pretty large market to get into. Though you might need to spend a reasonable sum on equipment (and land) if you choose this venture, but your sweet ₦500,000 can go far if you start small and choose a great location.

To conclude, let me inform you that when planning to start a business, it's important to choose an optimal business and also understand your target market. Also, take note that if you're starting a business in Nigeria, especially if you're investing ₦500,000 or above in it, it's essential to be cautious and assess the risks involved in the business to ensure you don't run into any problems.

Finally, the business ideas I discussed above are excellent ideas and should be profitable with thorough research and planning.

# Chapter 3

# Start Small and End Big

***Success is not final, Failure is not final: It is the courage to continue that counts***

-Winston Churchill-

Every big thing always starts small! You're the major and number one determining factor of your success and greatness when starting a business. The degree at which you will go solely depends on your ability to see ahead and see greatness in whatever you want to do.

Most people are not aware that it is not the amount of capital you start a business with that matters, but rather what you see about the business in future. Men don't rise by chance, they rise by what they believe in. If you believe in your capacity to succeed in your business, then trust me, that business will be great. You also need to understand this truth: what matters to you is not where you start from, it is rather where you are going.

Babies do not start walking the same day they are born, it takes some months. When a baby starts learning how to walk, he won't just start jumping from north to south. The baby will crawl for several weeks, after which he will start practicing how to lift one of his legs. When making attempts on lifting his leg, there will be several falls and rises.

After a while, the feet will eventually be firm on the ground and would be able to walk and run perfectly. This is the same in business, each will strive before they finally thrive! This is because, most times people need more time to build their trust in your brand, they need to see how consistent and diligent you are with your business, they want to see you show up every day, they want to see your work template. This is where the problems do come from most times - some business owners don't take time to build their brand. They are so quick to reach conclusions, especially when the business is not paying them enough, that it is not going to be big, and so they quit! Many businesses have shut down because their owners couldn't savor the moment and anticipate the success of their business. An individual who has problem with building a company cannot be a successful business owner, because it takes more time, patience, and consistency to grow a successful business.

You need to also understand at this juncture that when starting a business, you don't need to start with millions of money, especially when you are not financially buoyant enough. In fact, it is okay to start from the scratch even if you have all the money on you, this will enable you to learn in the process. You will discover the growth process and know what will work and not work for you.

## The Principle of Focus!

You want to build a long-term and successful business? Buy enough dose of focus. The ability to remain focused is one of the major principles that will guide you to success as a business owner. A focused business owner is a successful business owner. When you fix your attention on the right thing, then trust me, the right opportunity will come your way which will birth unto you your desired result. Focus breeds effectiveness, you can't do without it. To be focused means to be driven towards a particular direction or goal.

So, the question you should ask yourself right now is, "What is my goal as a business owner?" If you can understand what your goals are, that will set you up on track and keep you steady in any uncertain situation. Therefore, you should be driven by the future of your business. Your success tomorrow depends on your focus today. Starting small is great, but focusing on where you are heading is the greatest. Your beginning is not what matters after all, your end is. This means, you must focus on the end, I mean the end of your business. Some business names on the lips of people today became successful because they took their focus principle very seriously.

One of the advantages of focus is that it will keep attracting you to your desired end. You will be amazed at the result you will get when you can be focus-driven. As an entrepreneur, it is shocking to see how many entrepreneurs continue to get in their own way of success by focusing on the wrong things in business. There's no reason to make success hard when it's easy.

- ***Focus on what you can do and keep going to gain momentum:*** That is, focus on the easy parts first, then come back to the difficult aspects of building your business. Hopefully, by then, you'd have built up enough momentum that will keep your productive focus strong.

- ***Focus on activities that create results:*** Improve your focus on the day-to-day basic business activities you do best, from which you produce extraordinary results. If you don't, you'll create higher stress levels and may experience burnout. When you spend most of your time and energy doing the business tasks, you're brilliant at and allow others (like employees or sub-contractors) to do the rest, you reap the biggest rewards. In essence, what I am saying is, don't try to be everything, and don't do everything. Know your strengths and weaknesses. It is not a crime when you don't know everything, because of course, you are not omnipotent. It's okay not to know, it's okay to have weaknesses, though you shouldn't allow them to prevent you from making something meaningful out of your business.

For instance, don't try building a website unless you're a webmaster, and don't try learning technical skills if that isn't the best use of your time. Outsource those things instead, and focus on running your business so it can grow and prosper. To move faster and effectively in your business, you need other people to survive. These people are called team members. Hire them to work with and for you. You will need more hands to carry you through if you will ever go far and faster, source for more hands and focus more on your areas of strength. If not great at sending e-mails to customers/clients, you will do well to hire someone to do that on your behalf; if you are not good at graphic designing, get a graphic designer to work with you, and you pay them based on commission. This alone can make you achieve or earn ten times more than what you are currently earning.

- ***Focus on what works for you:*** You see, one of the easiest ways to be successful as a business owner is to know what works for you and stay focused on it, rather than what won't work. It is what works for you that will bring you success. Don't get fixated on what you don't know at first, you'll just get frustrated and stuck. A lot of business owners want to do what others are doing; well, it's not a bad idea to build on other people's ideas, but make sure you understand the idea, and be ready to stay on it such that you get hooked till the end.

- ***Multitask mindfully:*** Mindful multitasking allows you to stop reacting to distractions, such as the automatic reflex to answer the phone or read an incoming text. It allows you to focus on the actions that provide the best results and disregard everything else. After you set your intentions or goals for the day, create a to-do list that you can tackle using mindful multitasking, allowing yourself to be present in each action you would take for the day. This is so important for you to take note of as it really matters. I just want you to understand that you don't need to mind everything that happens around you. This is the principle of *mind your business*. Learn to mind your *business*, don't attend to phone calls when you are attending to clients or customers, don't eat while preparing letters, don't be bombarded with so many activities that will make you feel useless at the end of the day.

As earlier discussed in the previous point, learn to delegate tasks instead of doing it all. So many business owners are not succeeding because they don't understand this simple principle. Mind your business and own your space. The key to multitasking is to do it *strategically* and mindfully. Mindful multitasking means that you check in with yourself and determine how you need to focus in each new situation at a given period of time.

- ***Focus on developing one big project at a time:*** Don't forget that this chapter is discussing how to start your business in small, but end it in big. Good! As each and every single thought and principle is important to your business success, I also need to remind you that the principle of focus will take your business to places you won't imagine, if you can just get your mind on these principles.

Don't try to start multiple projects at once—it fragments focus and time. Entrepreneurs are creative people, often with many good business ideas, and it's hard turning off the desire to act on multiple ideas all at once. However, if you split your attention between more than one big project at a time, you'll run into trouble completing anything at all. You're going to need all your energy and focus to get your one new project off the ground. In essence, when you are trying to grow, improve or scale up your business, you must focus on one developmental idea at a time. Don't try to implement all ideas, this may be detrimental to the growth of your business. I definitely understand that as a business owner, you are prone to have so many ideas running back and forth in your mind, but don't ever be tempted to run all at once. Rather, execute one idea at a given time. If you are able to do that, believe me, your business will scale higher in no time.

## Ways to Focus on Growing Your Business

You are permitted to start small, but you're not permitted to end small. You are rather permitted to soar high and end big!

You can't grow a business until you have a clear vision of where you want it to go. Every great man you see out there is a millionaire. They are not necessarily people who were born with a silver spoon, nor are they people who started their businesses with millions of naira. Some of them started with few resources, some even started all alone without any staff working with them, but with a clear vision, they were able to start with just a leap of their faith in action and scale through.

So, when you're starting a business, you need to come to reality and be sincere with yourself.

Your sincerity should prompt you to ask an important question: what does it really take to grow a business? Unless you ask this sincere question and you give an answer to your quest, you may not move your business to any length or level before it dies.

You should also deliberately keep your eye on the big picture. Where do you see your business in the next five or ten years? What you see is what you will pursue. If you see nothing, you will pursue nothing. This is true, because I have come to realize that one of the main reasons businesses don't move is because their visioners aren't seeing the big picture. They lack foresight about where their business should be in few years to come. I can guarantee that your business will move if you can develop a specific vision for it and for yourself.

Growth is not automatic, it's a gradual process, and if you cannot see clearly, you won't get there early.

When it comes to succeeding in business, it doesn't happen by luck. You won't be successful because you met the right person or had a great referral. If you have zero respect for aim, or lack great vision for your business, it will be pretty hard to grow.

- ***Create your vision:*** As discussed earlier, vision is the vehicle that will drive you from where you are right now to where you originally belong. Vision will always show you where you ought to be; where you are will not always be where you should be. Many are where they are right now because they don't have a workable vision. If your business must succeed and have great sustainability, you must be visionary. A visionary man is unstoppable. Your business will thrive if you would develop a workable vision and run with it.

Most business owners wander through years without the knowledge of their destination. They do not know what they are creating, more like starting a vehicle without the direction. It is only a working vision that will keep your business alive and on track. You need to ascertain where you want your business to be in the next twenty, thirty, forty or whatever years you decide to go. I can't decide that for you, only you can do that.

Whatever vision you want to set for yourself, you must believe that it is achievable and can also survive. If you are presently struggling with your business, it's fine, especially if your business is still very young. But, see into the future and move with what you're seeing, because you won't always remain where you are at the moment. However, ask yourself these important questions if you want to develop a workable vision. They will act as a guide and an impetus for you. They may appear tough, but you still have to answer them, if you must grow.

a. *How big do I want my company to be?*
b. *What is my company known for? What do I want it to be known for?*
c. *How do I want my employees to feel about their jobs?*
d. *What industries do we want to work in?*
e. *What will my role be?*
f. *What will our everyday workload look like?*
g. *How do we measure success?*

These questions aren't new. They are questions successful business owners also asked. Countless business planning books and websites ask similar questions, if not the same. The answers, your answers – will provide the insight you need for your business vision.

- ***Know where you stand:*** Now that you have a vision, it is not enough; you need a detailed map – “a plan”. To create that, knowing where you stand today is the prerequisite. This has to do with measuring your present growth level, and that will make it easy to know where you want to go tomorrow. To grow your business from level one to ten, you must know and agree that it is presently in level one. You won’t grow if you can’t ascertain your current level.

Just as you asked yourself previously, you also need to answer the following questions:

- *Which of our products and services are successful?*
- *How profitable are they?*
- *What is their market share?*
- *How efficiently are we operating?*
- *Are we making the best use of technology and automation to get the job done?*
- *Are there areas we can save time?*
- *Do we have the resources in place to maintain our current business level and grow/expand?*

Having an accurate picture of the current operations and finances will help you determine the next steps to take to grow your business.

- ***Create the map to meet your vision***: Vision mapping is the process of creating a detailed mind map of the goals and dreams that you have for your business. Vision maps are a powerful tool that help you to create a personal vision and a detailed plan for your business. You can then use them to help businesses stay accountable to your vision. Without a solid vision map, you may not understand how you should go after your vision. Akin to a normal map, it is the vision map that will guide, act as your instructor, and give you plans on how to get your business growing from small to big.

Vision maps clearly show where you are, where you want to be, and what specific steps you need to take to get there. They also highlight the challenges you expect to encounter and the support you have to help you along the way. Like vision boards, your business vision map should also use visual elements to help paint a vivid picture of your vision.

Your vision maps are illustrations that are both image and text heavy, and their main purpose is to tell a story. They describe the current environments, complex future states, or plans and proposals on a single, placemat-sized sheet of paper. Vision mapping is writing a clear and specific vision with a detailed road map to achieving the vision, very similar to goal setting. It can help people accomplish their achievements and actually develop a plan on how to accomplish those achievements in a step-by-step journey. They may often involve some sort of visual travel plan, such as a road or a pathway to show from the starting point to the end goal with clear visual stops along the way.

Once you know what you're trying to achieve and understand what's happening in your business, you need to create the vision plan. Use the financial reports you've gathered to check your margins. Then, you need to ask yourself this important question: "Are we profitable?" If your answer is "No", make an effort to increase your business revenue by the road map you're creating and get the ball rolling.

Also, do competitive research to determine if your pricing is in line with your competitors. Then, ask yourself, "Is it time to raise our prices?" A small increase in pricing can make a huge improvement to the bottom line.

Believe me, your business will be highly successful if you can be intentional about your growth process, if you can create a workable vision and if you can plan how to get your vision achieved.

## Grow Business with Your Current Clients

Your current clients' perceptions can make or break your business. If you would love your business to grow, learn to deliver excellent and quality services. You must focus on your clients, not on yourself alone. Not even on the money or profit you want to gain, but rather on the quality experiences they will have when they do business with you. With this, they will quickly sing your praises on social media and herald you to the world even faster. Fast growth depends on making your current and potential customers happy.

Compared to large companies, small businesses are nimble and often better to see, anticipate, and respond to their customers' needs. The most successful small-business exploit is done by bringing new and innovative products and services to market more quickly and developing and nurturing long-term customer relationships. Dennis Tanjeloff, president and CEO of Astro Gallery of Gems said listening to your customers and giving them what they want is of utmost importance. So, for your business to grow, you need to see to it that you grow in relating well with your clients/customers. Know what they want and give them what they want, because this does not have much to do with you or what you feel, you need to listen to the heart cry of your clients.

It is less expensive to keep clients than to acquire new ones. Upselling to a current client who knows and trusts you is also much easier. Find their pain points and determine where else you can help them. Do you need to change your service levels, add additional products, or even create a passive income stream leveraging on a relationship with current clients?

## Stages of Business Growth

Every new business or start-up, big or small, goes through some stages of growth. These phases include existence, survival, and success. All stages of small business growth come with challenges that every company would have to overcome. Knowing where your business is in the cycle can help you see the solutions you need to implement, create growth strategies, and plan for the future. Whether you're still toying with a business idea or have already taken the plunge into entrepreneurship, this guide will give you a bird's eye view of the stages of starting and growing a business.

***Stage 1: Existence or the start-up stage***

Once you have a plan in place, it's time to put it into action, kicking off to the next stage of business growth: the start-up stage. During this time, you will test the viability of your big ideas as well as the effectiveness of your capabilities. This stage can represent a series of make-or-break moments for many small business owners.

In the existence stage, also called the start-up phase, the company's business structure is simple. For the most part, the owner manages the operations or performs all important operating activities. At this point, in the absence of investors, the owner is also the one funding the whole venture. For many, especially solo entrepreneurs, formal planning such as profit forecasting for the company is at a bare minimum. For the best potential for success, the owner should do market research and create a business plan.

Having the necessary capital is critical in this stage. The business needs funding to develop a viable product, deliver the product or service offerings to customers, and cover daily operating expenses - this is why running out of money is a small business's biggest risk.

Also, remember that at this stage, the brand is still trying to acquire new customers. So, even if the business has revenue, there probably isn't much in terms of profits. To survive the existence stage, entrepreneurs should learn about available options for raising money or finding investors to ensure they'll have the cash on hand to make their vision for their business happen.

***Stage 2: Survival***

Survival is the next phase following the existence stage. At this point, the business has proven that it's a viable brand; it has found a market for its products or services and has acquired customers. Also, most companies in this stage still operate with a simple structure. Even if the company now has employees, the owner oversees and makes the major decisions for the business. They may not have any systems in place for hiring practices, marketing models, etc. In addition, some businesses may still be operating with minimal formal planning, with the goals for the company existing only in the mind of the owner.

After the initial excitement of breaking into a market, which is an accomplishment itself, the strategy at this stage of growth is to survive—which means the business needs to start looking for ways to make money consistently. Most companies expect not to make much, if any, profit in the first few years of operation, but they should at least break even and generate enough revenue to cover expenses and replace capital assets as they wear out. The alternative is running out of money, with the end result being either selling the company or selling its assets.

***Stage 3: Success***

The third stage of business growth is success. At this maturity phase, the company is thriving. It has established a strong presence in the industry to ensure consistent profits. Plus, as a mature business, it has the brand recognition and size to be financially healthy.

At this stage, the business would have grown enough to add more employees and probably a couple of managers. The brand might even be completely separate from the owner at this point. Accounting practices, marketing plans, and production systems would also be in place. With other skilled leaders in place, the owner won't need to supervise every aspect of the company.

Now that the business has become profitable and achieved success, the main strategy is to keep the company stable and profitable and to manage cash flow so it can weather rough times. The company can cruise in this place indefinitely as long as there are no disruptions in the industry or management issues.

When your company reaches the maturity stage, it's the result of a lot of hard work and perseverance, along with a business idea that has proven its worth. Through strategic planning and maneuvering, you and your team created the perfect climate for success, helping you to evolve from a start-up to industry standard bearer. It's now, for mature businesses, that the importance of growth merges with the need for retention and other business interests.

Although maturity is considered a final stage for business growth, it is not a finish line or a time to sit back, put the evolving strategies and planning aside and coast along for years to come. Businesses are living, breathing entities. Long-term success requires inspiration, continued commitment, and an ability to meet the needs of an ever-changing world and customer base with new products and ideas. Stagnation, at this point, invites greater competition and makes reacting to market trends more cumbersome.

## Chapter 4

# Understanding Risk and Its Great Rewards

*The biggest risk is not taking risk. In a world that is changing quickly, the only*

***strategy that is guaranteed to fail is not taking risk.***

-Mark Zukerberg-

No business can survive if the owner does not take any risk. Risk is life and life is risk. Going out in the morning takes risk, coming back in the night takes risk, eating and drinking take risk, virtually everything you'll ever do in your life takes risk. Starting a business in the first place takes some levels of risk, and if you cannot take them, business is not for you. If you are afraid to fail, afraid to make mistakes, or afraid to make some firm decisions about your business and company, then don't think about doing business at all.

When you are coming into the business world, you must know exactly what you want and must be ready to sacrifice everything your business would need to survive. Hence, you should know that business is for the stronghearted, because your business may fail or possibly succeed. However, have the positive mind that you will succeed anyways.

In business, taking risks is inevitable. It is a necessary evil. You can't do without it, you must take it. A risk can bring a downfall to the whole business, while another on the other hand can take the business to its next phase. Risks are factors that an organization encounters that may lower its profits or cause it to fail. Sources of risk can be external, such as changes in what consumers want, changes in competitor behavior, external economic factors, government rules or regulations and so on. They can also be internal such as decisions made by management or the executive team. Any risk (whether external or internal) made by a business owner can either make or mar its progress, this is why a company must understand risk and which type to take at a particular period of time.

You should understand now that no company can completely avoid risks, especially since most risk factors are external. However, businesses can put risk management strategies into place. These strategies can be used to both reduce risks and mitigate the impact(s) when they arise. By documenting the sources of risk and creating a strategic plan that can be repeated, businesses can reduce the overall impact of risk and deal with it more efficiently and effectively in the future.

Business risks are any type of potential threat to an organization's profits, overarching goals, or overall safety. Many entrepreneurs are scared of taking one because they are not ready to make a difference. Changing of brand name, logo, consumer's taste, and so on are all risks, because you may not in any way understand what your clients or consumers really want at a time. Even when you have done your market research, analysis, and studies, you may still fall short in some areas and one mistake committed by you can destroy your years of plans and investment.

Like I noted the other time, there are both internal and external risks to consider, and businesses have been managing them for years. Some examples of business risks may include economic changes, political dynamic switches, and everyday business-associated risks such as employees' health and safety. The type of risks that an organization has can fluctuate depending on the type of business, not all organizations have the same business risks. As time goes on, new risks present themselves, so it is important to anticipate and prepare for both seen and unforeseen risks.

## Understanding Risk

The understanding of risk differs, the methods of assessment and management also differ. Likewise, its descriptions and even definitions differ in different practice areas such as business, economics, environment, finance, information technology, health, insurance, safety, security, and so on. As an individual who wants to survive and be successful in business, you must understand what risk is all about.

Now, let me start by explaining what risk is, this will give you a grounding about it. Risk is the probability that an accidental phenomenon produces at any given point in time. You see, in every business, whether a small retail store or a big manufacturing company, there are common challenges, either money problems, fire outbreak, damages, or vehicle accidents. Losses can also occur as a result of defective products, etc. An organization faces business risk when it is exposed to a situation that can lead to decreased profits or even bankruptcy.

## What is Business Risk?

There is a risk to every business decision you make. So, instead of relying on gut instinct, it's a good idea to use risk management to guide your decisions. You need to understand what risk management is and the types of risk that could affect your business

Business risks refer to internal and external factors that can lower a company's profits or lead it to fail. They are factors that threaten your ability to operate, leading to loss of profits or business failure. From start-ups to multinational corporations in every industry imaginable, all are exposed to threats that can harm their success.

While you can't eliminate the possibility of risk, you can take steps to mitigate its presence or impact on your business.

Risk management helps you make better business decisions. It involves reducing the things that could have a negative effect on your business. For example, reducing the risk of injury through safety procedures. You can also look for opportunities that could have a positive impact on your business.

## Types of Business Risks

Building a business requires risks. Running one takes hard work, which can reap the rewards of customers, revenue, and satisfaction. While success is the ultimate goal, some risks are more dangerous than others and may stop you from achieving your goals. When it comes to risk management, there are steps you can take, however. Here are seven types of business risk you may want to address in your company.

***Financial Risk***

The first type of risk that every business faces is financial risk. This includes not having enough money to pay for goods or services needed by your company. The amount of money you need to cover any given period of time depends on many factors, including the size of your company, how much revenue it generates, what expenses it incurs, and whether or not there are unexpected costs associated with a particular project. In other words, financial risk is the possibility of losing money on an investment or business venture. Some more common and distinct financial risks include credit risk, liquidity risk, and operational risk. Financial risk is a type of danger that can result in the loss of capital to interested parties. Business owners face it when they make decisions that may jeopardize their income or ability to pay a debt they have assumed. What you need to understand as a business owner is that financial risks are everywhere, on several occasions, they are inevitable. They come in many shapes and sizes, affecting nearly everyone. You should be aware of its presence. Knowing the dangers and how to protect your business will not eliminate it, but it can mitigate the harm and reduce the chances of a negative outcome.

At some point in every business, there would be a need to upgrade and build the business to achieve more feats. Hence, it is expensive to build a business from the ground up. At some point in any company's life, the business may need to seek outside capital to grow. This need for funding creates a financial risk to both the business and to any investor or stakeholder who has invested in the company.

### *Cultural Risk*

If you will ever be a successful business owner, you must put locality into consideration. You must be able to do a thorough local feasibility study. This will enable you to know what your localities want and what they do not want. Some businesses have failed due to cultural differences, for instance, selling Bibles in a community where there are about 90% of Muslims. If you are selling a generator for power supply in a country where they seldom have power outages, then you are in for a rude shock.

Cultural risk refers to the potential of a company's operations in a country to struggle because of differences in language, customs, norms, and customer preferences. It involves the effects of cultural diversity on a group of people. Some examples of cultural risk include racism, sexism, homophobia, xenophobia, etc. One way to manage it is to make sure that you hire diverse teams. This ensures that you have a wide range of perspectives regarding decision-making.

Here are some cultural risks to consider: failing to adapt your business model to the local market, failing to recognize regional differences in cultures, failing to adapt your management practices across different cultures.

### *Operational Risk*

Operational risk is another major concern for companies. It refers to the possibility of something going wrong during normal operations. Operational risk is also the risk of loss as a result of ineffective or failed internal processes, people, systems, or external events which can disrupt the flow of business operations. For example, if you are running out of product on your shelves, machine breakdown, or excessive high defect rate, then you are facing operational risk. It also includes human errors, technical errors and gaps in operational processes, uncontrollable events, and intentional fraud.

One of the ways by which you can mitigate operational risk as a business owner is to train yourself and employees about risk and its management, because operational risk, on most occasions, happens as a result of miscommunication or mishandling of resources within the company or organization. If your team members are not well-informed about the equipment they are using or if they are not in good terms with one other, it can cause an effective company to become ineffective.

### *Organizational Risk*

Anything that threatens a company's ability to achieve its financial goals is considered a business risk. Organizational risk is anything that generates uncertainty within an enterprise. Business leaders concern themselves with organizational risk because it has a direct impact on the financial stability of their business. It also includes poor leadership, ineffective communication, and a lack of cooperation within the organization.

Some common examples of organizational risk include:

- *Product launch:* Launching a new product or starting a new business in an unknown land often requires a great deal of time and money, and introduces risk in a business because you don't know whether the product or business will be successful.

- *Natural disasters:* Many businesses are at risk of being affected by a natural disaster such as a hurricane damaging a building or an earthquake disrupting the supply chain.

- *Communication:* When a business relies on a third-party system for communication, they're entrusting an essential element of their business to another company.
- *Regulation compliance:* Failure to meet government regulations could mean fines, lawsuits, or damage to the business's reputation. In some countries, if you start any business without formal registration, it may be held down.

***Reputational Risk***

Reputational risk is any sort of threat or danger that can damage the good standing of your business and negatively impact your reputation with consumers and overall business success. In other words, it refers to the damage that could be done to an organization or business reputation. This risk is typically unexpected and can occur with little to no warning; it includes both negative and positive effects. A negative effect might be losing customers due to poor customer service, while a positive effect would be gaining new customers due to good customer service.

Reputation risk can happen by your inability to consistently meet customer needs or falling short of customer expectations, poor working conditions for employees or exploitative working conditions, business leaders with negative reputations or who develop negative reputations through specific actions, employees poorly representing your brand or business to others, negative social media posts by those associated with your business, and so on.

Every business has some forms of risk. However, each business will face different types of risks depending on their industry. To mitigate these risks, companies must understand them thoroughly and take steps to minimize them.

**How You Can Manage Risk in Your Business**

Business risk originates from different areas, but the main ones are from the internal and external sources. The best way for a business to manage risk is to evaluate risk factors and make contingency plans on how to deal with it when and if it presents itself. Planning for risks is the main theme of risk management, but you cannot plan for everything. Hence, managing risks also has a lot to do with how you react when they arise. As a business owner who desires success in his business, you must know how to manage the effects of risk on your business. Risks are inevitable, but they can be minimized.

Risk management has always been an important tool in running any business, particularly when a market experiences a downturn. In any economic environment, an unexpected surprise can destroy your business in one fell swoop if you don't have the right risk management strategies in place to prevent or at least mitigate the damage from that risk.

To prevent or manage risk in your business, do the following:

- ***Write a business plan****:* The process of writing and putting together a business plan is a vital step to assessing, evaluating, and planning for the risks of running a business from the various standpoints of the business. This includes operations, finance, and marketing. Writing a business plan will help you see and probably discover what will effectively work for your business and what will not work.

- ***Train employees:*** Avoiding risks and knowing how to deal with the risk if it occurs can help the business avoid further damage or exposing itself to risk in the first place. For example, if your business deals with a heavy machine, you may want to have each of your employees go for a special training. This will enable them to get more exposure, insights, and knowledge about what they are supposed to do. Some big organizations send their employees for training which can last for days or even weeks. As a business owner, I strongly advise that you go for training if you want to reduce the cost of risk in your organization.

- ***Determine insurance needs and obtain coverage:*** Most businesses carry liability insurance or insure the building and contents with which the business operates. Depending on the business activities, you need to determine the other types of insurance and obtain the correct coverage for your business.

  For example, a tile installation business should carry liability insurance in case a worker gets injured while installing tiles. A real estate business or legal business may obtain an errors and omissions insurance policy in case a client sues for a professional wrongdoing.

- ***Write a risk management plan:*** Separate from your business plan, write a risk management plan which lists all of the possible risks that can affect the business. The plan also lists the steps, procedures, and ways in which the business intends on dealing with each risk as it arises. For example, if your business is located in an area of the country prone to hurricanes, then you may have a hurricane preparation plan on how you can minimize the risks associated with this type of weather to your business. Begin by finding out about risk management practices and how you can use them. You should also talk to others involved in your business (including your employees and customers) to decide on the best way to manage risk in your business.

Before you decide on what to do, you'll need to work out what your risks are and which ones are most urgent, which means, you need to

- *Identify*: work out what risks your business could face;
- *Analyze:* find the level of the risks and which ones are most urgent;
- *Evaluate:* compare the risk against set risk criteria to decide what to do.

**Great Rewards in Taking Risk**

Every successful business owner and entrepreneur took great risks to become who they are today. Most of them resigned from their well-paid jobs, most left their comfort zone, and so on. Having the courage to break out of your comfort zone can feel scary, but depending on how you approach a situation, you can bring more joy into your life than you deem possible.

Risk taking can uncover vulnerability, imperfection, and embarrassment. However, the rewards of a calculated risk may lead to feeling like and becoming a successful person. However, you can define that. Practicing with small risks each day can help you to build a template for taking more and bigger risks as you go. And, when you take small risks often, you would feel more confident when it is time to take a big risk. You may start to understand and experience how taking risks can be rewarding in your life. If you try and fail repetitively, it can be discouraging. It may even feel like you are a failure. However, you are not a failure because a risk you took failed. Adapting a growth mindset (one in which we learn from failure and become stronger and grow more as a person) shifts the focus from shame and embarrassment to "what can I learn from this?", so that you can continue to move forward. It's difficult to isolate the disappointment of one event if you don't identify as a risk taker. However, when you shift your perspective, you may see benefits with risk taking.

As an entrepreneur, if you want to achieve the life you've always dreamed of, you'll have to start taking positive, calculated risks. It is absolutely necessary to take chances to achieve anything great in life, however many are scared to take the initial leap. As with any risk, there is always something at stake. In most instances, when it comes to your business, you stand to lose money, time, and your reputation, which are also the very same things you stand to gain! The benefits of taking risks will enrich your life and make your business or career much more rewarding.

## The Benefits of Taking Risks

It's a known fact that over thirty percent of start-ups fail within two years. This isn't meant to scare you into avoiding starting your own business, but to showcase the reality of entrepreneurship. Successful entrepreneurship involves taking risks. Countless entrepreneurs have taken risks to get their businesses to where they are now. Taking risks, however, does not mean going into business blindly and then expecting great results. Instead, successfully approaching risks requires careful planning and an underlying strategy.

Take note of the following:

- ***Taking risks will open you up to new challenges and opportunities:*** In fact, taking risks can push you to learn a new skill, such as public speaking, which comes in handy as a business owner.

- ***Taking risks empowers you to establish new limits in your mind:*** We all have boundaries or a comfort zone where we'd like to stay and many have misconstrued visions of what we think we deserve or are capable of accomplishing. When you take risks, you can eradicate that thinking, establish new boundaries, and improve your outlook on life and your ability to achieve on high levels.

- ***Taking risks can cause you to become more creative:*** When you put yourself out on a limb, with a no-excuse approach, your natural problem-solving skills kick in and you're open to new ideas as well as willing to try something new.

- *Taking risks can result in a positive outcome.* Not every life step can be carefully planned out. You'll never know if you can succeed unless you venture out into new territory. Is there a risk involved in doing something totally new? Sure. But the reward is there too. When you give it your best shot and put all that you can into achieving the goal, you are more likely to make it happen.

- *Taking risks help you to clearly define what you really want.* Calculated risks are taken with careful thoughts, yet the fact that you are taking a risk pushes you to make things work. Surely, you will first have to determine if the reward is something you really want enough to make you take the chance. If it is, then move ahead and don't look back.

Once you have become accustomed to taking risks, you break free from the average way of living and thinking. Instead of fighting to stay safe, you rather gain the momentum and confidence needed to welcome new opportunities in your career or business. Risks build your self-confidence and self-respect, empowering you to feel stronger in taking on new endeavors. When you are open to new challenges, you position yourself to profit a whole lot more than you would just by staying the same.

Taking chances requires some blind trust in most cases. Nothing is really guaranteed. However, you have to trust your instincts. Sometimes your gut is leading you down on an unknown path, but deep inside you know that something big is on the other side. Go for it, you'll never know all you can accomplish until you do something you've never done. Take the risk today and you'll step into some of your biggest rewards.

## Chapter 5

# Understanding Your Clients/Customers

---

***Your most unhappy customers are your greatest source of learning***

---

-Bill Gates-

As a business owner, your clients are your biggest asset. Without a strong customer base, a business will fall apart. Although, acquiring new customers may be difficult, it is necessary for business growth. Maintaining good relationships with your current customers is just as important as your business name and brand. In fact, it costs organizations six to seven times more to attract a new client than it does to retain a current one. Understanding your clients' needs and being able to meet their demands will give your business a competitive edge. The ability to read between the lines, know what your clients require from you, and anticipate this need is a vital part of meeting stakeholder expectations and maintaining happy and healthy relationships.

While it may not be as straightforward as checking items off a list, learning how to identify your clients' underlying challenges and unspoken needs is a skill you can hone and improve.

As an entrepreneur, it should be obvious that understanding your clients is critical for the health of your business, but the question is how can you go about gaining meaningful insights? With data, of course! Businesses should be proactively gathering data about their clients whenever possible. Check up on their social media pages to see what kinds of conversations people are having with them and if possible, research your clients' websites to learn more about them. By dissecting your clients' needs, your organization will be more equipped to deliver offerings and customer service that are aligned with those needs. What's more? Knowing your customers enables your organization to create more targeted marketing strategies, maintain strong relationships with clients, and increase the existence value of clients.

If you don't understand the needs of your potential customers, you'll never close the sale to make them active customers. Once you have a customer, you must continue to understand and meet their ongoing needs or you won't retain the business. You need to know how to identify client's needs.

But, how do you ensure you address client needs in a way that advances your business? Let's look at five key tactics for understanding client needs and therefore meeting their expectations.

## Examples of Common Customer Needs

No two customers will have the exact same needs, but you're likely to run into some of these common ones repeatedly. When assessing how best you can help your next client, look out for the following:

- ***Transparency:*** This is another way of staying clear, consistent, and having open communication with the client. That could mean sending out regular updates, meeting with them frequently to receive feedback, or developing up-to-date timelines so they know when to expect your work.

- ***Availability:*** Clients with this need want to be able to access your team whenever they need. That may mean having a dedicated client service employee to interface with them, or simply staying on top of all emails and chats so that you never miss a message.

- ***Control:*** Some clients may want an extremely high level of involvement at all stages of the project, while others may only want to be involved with the essentials. Properly assessing (and sometimes reevaluating) how much or little control they want (or should have) over a project can be important.

- ***Trust:*** Closely related to control and transparency, trust is ultimately about how much confidence the client has in your abilities to meet their challenges. While every client would prefer to have complete confidence, this may not be possible. It will be up to you to properly assess their level of trust, then put processes in place that help you manage the relationship while also instilling confidence.

- ***Measurable results:*** This is when clients want to be able to see the impact of solving their core problems. Whether qualitative or quantitative, this will likely require your team to collect data throughout the length of your project that shows the results of your efforts.

## How to Understand Your Clients/Customers

To provide good customer service, you must first acknowledge your present and potential customers. You must also deliver on your promises to provide good customer service. On the other hand, great customer service entails getting to know your customers so well that you can foresee their desires and go above and beyond their expectations. It also requires that you foresee your customers' life cycle stages to anticipate any new needs as they progress through these stages. Below are my few points on how you can understand your customers.

- ***Determine the motivation of the customer:*** Customer motivation analysis can be a great source of new ideas. Essentially asking, "What task is the consumer attempting to get done?" can expose the anxieties and aspirations that motivate transactions. Whenever you notice a task that is not being handled well, for example, when a customer's main specifications aren't being satisfied or if there are impediments to consumption, you can start looking for economic reinvention and development prospects. This act of service won't only make your customers feel happy but will also make them come back to do business with you, and can earn you referrals to their friends and colleagues who may need your service in the future.

- ***Acquire a 360-degree view of your customers:*** To acquire a 360-degree view of your customers, you need to use syndicated research. While undertaking polls or examining data sources does appear like a logical step, you must go even further to get a complete picture. If you rely solely on consumer surveys or statistics from your website, you may end up with a subpar pool of data. Only your most engaged and favorable consumers will respond to surveys. Customer engagement is revealed by website statistics, but the needs and demands of potential consumers are not.

Third-party data that is syndicated can reach all potential customers, not just your present client base, and may reveal new trends. Using consumer research to assess whether moving into a prospective new market would be beneficial for your firm will help you examine the demand for your company's service or its products on numerous levels.

- ***Put yourself in your clients' shoes:*** Understanding your clients requires you to put yourself in their position and scrutinize any contact points where they interact with your company. Discussions, visits, and deliveries also fall under this category, and so does any online interactions, phone conversations, and emails too. Is your office dirty, your receptionist unpleasant, your website is difficult to explore, or emails going unopened? Any of these factors can lead to dissatisfaction among customers. Being kept waiting a long time is by far the most prevalent customer complaint. You run the risk of losing consumers if you take too long to reply to calls or fulfill orders. Customers, above all, expect you to hold your promises and deliver beyond their expectations.

As a small firm, you can focus on providing personalized service. You may make a customer's day if you remember their name and clearly remember your last interaction with them. They may even inform their friends about your excellent service standards.

Acknowledging your consumers and enhancing your service should be a priority for everyone in your company. From the entrance receptionist to the delivery team, everybody must strive to surpass client expectations.

- ***Ask your consumer's opinions:*** If you must succeed as a business owner, then you must make your clients or customers feel cherished by conducting a customer satisfaction questionnaire. You'll also learn something new, because this would expose you to some hidden truths you don't know. But, don't request a critique unless you're willing to change in response. Inform your customers of everything you've accomplished as an outcome of their comments when you make changes.

Well-constructed customer surveys can reveal information that you didn't realize, such as human elements like staff behavior. When people are unsatisfied, not everybody protests. Often, unhappy customers tell their acquaintances about their unpleasant experience and go somewhere else to do their shopping. You might not figure out where you're going astray until you discuss it with your customers ahead of time. Establish a customer engagement campaign in addition to seeking feedback to guarantee that you're staying in contact with them. You can pay heed and further inform them about what you would do if you have an effective customer interaction approach.

Your customers are the soul of your business, and you should never neglect the fact that you need to establish some understanding between you and them to keep your business alive in the long run.

## How to Treat Your Customers

How to treat customers is one of the difficult challenges in business because every person has their own unique needs and wants, but these general guidelines can help you avoid committing any major errors. By following these simple tips, you'll be able to create a better customer service experience that will increase both customer satisfaction and loyalty.

- ***Treat customers professionally:*** When it comes to treating customers professionally, there are few things you can do to make sure you're putting your best foot forward. Act politely and confidently. Be aware of your body language and make sure you're not crossing your arms or slouching. Be sure to smile and maintain eye contact. Make sure you've dressed appropriately if it is a video or an in-person interaction.

- ***Treat customers as individuals:*** Customers want personalized service. When you're interacting with them, take the time to learn their names and use them in your conversations. Ask questions about what they do and what they're interested in. Show genuine interest in who they are as a person, not just as a customer.

- ***Treat customers fairly and equally:*** When you treat customers equally and fairly, you can maintain a positive relationship with them even when you may not be telling them what they want to hear. Having standard guidelines for customer interactions can help to ensure that everyone is being treated the same and that no one feels like they're being given unfair treatment. Your business will succeed if customers notice you're not favoring an individual over others.

- ***Keep your promises to customers:*** As a business owner who wants to be a success in his business endeavors, when you promise to do something, make sure you follow through with it. Failing to keep your promises will only frustrate and annoy customers, and it can damage the trust you've built with them. Keep track of your commitments and make sure you're able to meet them in a timely manner.

- ***Avoid being judgmental or dismissive:*** Even if you may not agree with a customer's complaint, it's important to avoid being judgmental or dismissive. Instead, try to see their side of the issue and understand where they're coming from. Show them that you're willing to work with them to resolve the problem.

- ***Thank customers and provide incentives:*** At the end of the interaction, it is essential to thank the customer for their business. This is a small gesture that can mean a lot. Show your appreciation by providing them with an incentive to make them come back in the future. This could be in the form of a discount, freebie, or even just some words of encouragement.

- ***Take the time to properly resolve customer issues:*** When a customer has an issue, they want it to be resolved as quickly and efficiently as possible. But in some cases, rushing to a resolution can do more harm than good. If an issue is complex or requires more time to investigate, let the customer know that you're working on it and provide regular updates.

- ***Take responsibility for your mistakes:*** Customers will appreciate your honesty and integrity. When you make a mistake, take responsibility and own up to it. Apologize to the customer and explain what you're doing to correct the situation. Show them that you're taking their satisfaction seriously and that you value their business.

- ***Make sure customers feel appreciated and valued:*** One of the best ways to show customers that you appreciate them is to let them know. Let them know how you will change things based on their experience or suggestions. You can also make them feel appreciated with simple discounts or a shout-out on social media.

- ***Be more customer-centric and get on the same page with clients:*** The secret to loyal customer relationships isn't actually much of a secret at all, you just need to be able to tune in to their needs and deliver the results they want. Easier said than done? Perhaps. While there will always be hard-to-please clients, you will likely be able to please the vast majority by taking a more thorough, proactive approach to understanding their challenges and uncovering their needs, both implicit and explicit.

Although not all of the above strategies may be necessary for your next client engagement, the philosophy behind them, taking your time listening to your customers, and always looking for opportunities to improve, are how you can become more customer-centric.

## Chapter 6

# Managing Your Business Finance

***The price of success is hard work dedication to the job at hand, and the determination that whether we win or lose, we have applied the best of ourselves to the task at hand***

-Vince Lombardi-

No business owner likes being strapped for cash, but cash flow mismanagement happens. Money management is the process of handling your business's finances through budgeting, setting goals, tracking income and expenses, and investing. With a sound money management plan, you can avoid periods of negative cash flow and ensure your business is on track to turn a profit. Failing to manage money wisely can lead to problems like making late payments, running out of money, and not collecting in your accounts receivable.

Often, your small business is successful because of your expertise in making your product or providing your service. Unfortunately, you might not be an expert at the other important aspects of running a business, such as managing finances. If you don't have a lot of experience with managing business finances, it can be a challenge, but it's also crucial to the survival of your business. Note the following.

- ***Don't be afraid of loans:*** Loans can lead business owners to worry about the financial repercussions of failure. However, without the influx of capital you obtain from loans, you may face substantial challenges when trying to purchase equipment or grow your team. You can also use loan proceeds to boost your cash flow and thus face fewer issues in paying employees and suppliers on time. Plus, the best business loans come with terms and rates that many small business owners can easily accommodate.

- ***Pay yourself:*** If you are running a small or midsize business (SMB), it can be tempting to put everything into your day-to-day operations. After all, that extra capital can often go a long way in helping your business grow. Alexander Lowry, a professor and director of the Master of Science in Financial Analysis Program at Gordon College said small business owners shouldn't overlook their own role in the company and should compensate themselves accordingly. You want to ensure that your business and personal finances are in good shape.

"Many SMB owners, especially at the outset, neglect to pay themselves," he said. "They (believe) it's more important to get the business up and running and pay everyone else. But, if the business doesn't work out, you won't have ever paid yourself. Remember, you're part of the business, and you need to compensate yourself as much as you pay others."

- ***Focus on both expenditures and ROI:*** Measuring expenditures and return on investment (ROI) can give you a clear picture of which investments make sense and which may not worth continuing. Deborah Sweeney, CEO of My Corporation, said small business owners should be mindful of where they spend their money.

"Focus on the ROI that comes with each of your expenditures," she said. "Not doing this means that you can lose money on irrelevant or bad spending bets. Know where you are spending your hard-earned money and how that investment is paying off. If it isn't paying off, cut back and spend a bit more on the initiatives that do work for you and your business."

- ***Set up good financial habits:*** Establishing internal financial protocols, even if it's as simple as dedicating a set time to reviewing and updating financial information, can go a long way in protecting the financial health of your business. Keeping up with your finances can help you mitigate fraud or risk.

"As small business owners, we are often strapped for time, money and have vastly inferior technological capabilities, but it shouldn't prevent any small business owner from implementing some sort of internal control," Collado said. "Weak internal controls can lead to employee fraud or theft, and can potentially get you into legal problems if you or an employee are not abiding by certain laws."

- *Invest in growth.* It's important to set aside money and look into growth opportunities which can allow your business to thrive and move in a healthy financial direction. It is good that business owners should always keep an eye on the future. A small business that wants to continue to grow, innovate, and attract the best employees [should] demonstrate that they are willing to invest in the future. Customers will appreciate the increased level of service. Employees will appreciate that you are investing in the company and in their careers. And ultimately, you will create more value for your business than if you were just spending all your profits on personal matters.

- ***Separate business and personal funds:*** Do you have a separate bank account for your business? Even if you aren't required to separate business and personal funds, doing so is critical for money management sake. Plus, business bank statements are useful for tracking profitability, reconciling your books, and monitoring spending.

Mixing your personal and business funds can result in disorganized records, leading to overspending and missed growth opportunities. When you combine funds, tracking withdrawn and deposited business funds becomes difficult, making it challenging to monitor incoming and outgoing money. If your business and personal funds are in one account, you might be prone to dip into your business funds for personal expenses or vice versa.

## Managing Your Business Finance

It is important at this junction to discuss how you can set up your business finance, whether you are a small business owner or a big business owner. One of the things you will need is a separate bank account for your business and a good book-keeping system to help you track the records of your finances.

As a business owner who wants to be successful, you have to develop a routine for managing money in your business. For example, you can determine to do financial admin work on a weekly basis. This includes getting all your receipts or invoices and making proper calculations and documentation of them all in your company's book-keeping records. Once that is done, then you can now match what you have on your record with what you have in your bank statements. For instance, if your company purchases new equipment, definitely the money for the purchase will be withdrawn from your bank. Now, it is important to also have the transaction amount in your book record system. The same applies if your company makes sales of products/services and so on. If you must make something good out of your business, you must also take your financial records seriously. Recording your company's daily income and expenditure makes you more accountable and a better financial manager.

One of the reasons you must have this routine is so that you can keep an updated description of your statements, because most times, bank statements are not always helpful. Mismanagement of finances has made a lot of businesses wind up. Some were not aware of the importance of keeping daily income and expenditure record, some took out loans that couldn't be repaid by the company, while some happened due to low financial IQ.

If you want your business to earn and save more, separate your personal financial burden from that of the company. In other words, don't put personal loads and financial burden on the company's finances. A lot of business owners make this abnormal mistake a lot of times. Normally, as a business owner, if you want to manage your business money, then you must also be on your company's payroll, which means the company should pay you a certain amount of salary. If the company's financial strength is not enough to pay you yet, then you need to know how much stipend you will be taking for yourself, probably on a weekly or monthly basis. Don't spend your business funds anyhow. Because you feel it belongs to you doesn't give you the freedom to use it the way you like. If you spend it in a frivolous manner, you will soon run your business into liquidation.

### Gain Financial Education

As a business owner, being financially literate shouldn't be a negotiation for you. Financial literacy is the ability to understand and make use of a variety of financial skills, including personal financial management, budgeting, and investing. It also means comprehending certain financial principles and concepts, such as the time value of money, compound interest, managing debt, and financial planning.

Achieving financial literacy can help businesses to avoid making poor financial decisions. It can help them become self-sufficient and achieve financial stability. Key steps to attaining financial literacy include learning how to create a budget, how to track spending, pay off your debts, and also staff salaries. Educating yourself on these topics also involves learning how money works, setting and achieving financial goals, becoming aware of unethical/discriminatory financial practices, and managing financial challenges that life throws your way.

## How to Gain Financial Education

There are some incredible steps you can take to become educated financially. It is not enough to make money; that you make enough doesn't mean you're educated financially. So many people are wealthy, but lack financial education. There are business owners who know absolutely nothing about money and finances, these people do fall into financial traps in the future. For you not to be a victim of financial traps, I have listed below some of the steps you can take to become financially educated.

- ***Use financial management tools:*** One of the important steps you can take to gain literacy in finance is to use financial management tools. There are many services available online, numerous free online financial courses and tools you can engage with. I can recommend that you see some YouTube videos that discuss finances.

Also, get *Rich Dad, Poor Dad*, a powerful book on finance, business, and money by Robert Kiyosaki. You may as well want to source for resources such as podcasts and webinars that teach financial literacy, or take a college course in personal finance for a more guided learning approach.

These among many are financial tools that can help you build your business finance and also manage it appropriately.

- ***Ask questions.*** A financial advisor can answer your questions about how to handle money, credits, and debts. They can evaluate your specific and current situation and make recommendations on how to consolidate and manage your finances to pay off your debts. You might also ask a friend or family member who works in a finance organization or who has significant personal experience managing finances for help with your own financial assets.

- ***Invest in retirement***. As a business owner, you must have the foresight to look into the future and invest in it. Being financially literate also means understanding how to plan your future financial life and prepare for retirement. This is one of the mistakes most business owners do make. They never plan for the future; they won't save, nor put money aside for future endeavors. You need to set aside some percentage of your income for your retirement, so that you don't fall into a financial mess in the future.

  Saving for retirement can take a lifetime of planning and contributions, so it's important to start learning as soon as possible.

- ***Learn to budget:*** Another crucial step is to learn budgeting. Budgeting is one of those key components of literacy in finance. Learning to create and manage a budget allows you to pay down or avoid debt, save money, and plan for your future. Once you understand how to use money management tools and understand basic financial concepts, you can start applying them first with a personal budget. Create a budget for your basic expenses and start tracking spending, incomes, and fixed expenses. Set strict limits for spending and review your budget monthly.

- ***Seek out a mentor:*** Another simple way to increase one's financial literacy is getting a mentor who can guide you on setting budgets, sticking to costs, and improving cash flow and profitability. Financial mentors provide a one-on-one service focused on financial well-being. A mentor will support you to make the right connections with other business owners, local networks, and social services to ensure you are in the right circle.

The mentor can be a single person or people like successful entrepreneurs who are a stage ahead of you. You can even pay to get a mentor for yourself.

Chapter 7

# Don't Quit Your Business

---

***If you don't build your dream, someone else will hire you to help them build theirs***

---

-Dhirubhai Ambani-

It may be challenging to start your business and it may get harder as you work your way up to achieve success. You may lose the drive and motivation along the way and even think of giving up. What you need to do is think about the reason why you decided to get your business started in the first place. Who will benefit from this? How significant is it for you, and why should you do this? Your answers to the questions will make you persevere and not give up.

Real success does not happen in the blink of an eye. You can't just wish to accomplish something and expect that it will come quickly. Real success comes with pains, winning over trials, overcoming obstacles, and persevering despite various failures. Today's most successful people have shown us how determination and belief in oneself can lead one to massive success. We should never develop an "I give up" attitude.

**Don't Quit!**

In life, there will always be the easy and the difficult paths. Depending on the circumstances, one gets to know which to follow. But, one thing is certain when it comes to entrepreneurship - so many hard decisions need to be made.

A lot of times, when a founder decides to quit altogether, it is because quitting seems to be the easy way out. A founder who will always budge at the littlest challenge is miles away from realizing what true entrepreneurship is all about. Perhaps it is necessary to reset priorities and ask if truly entrepreneurship is meant for you or simply just make do with paid employment.

## Benefits of Not Quitting Your Business

The harder something is, the stronger you will become. Maybe not physically, but mentally. Your mindset grows just like a muscle, so it is great to have some challenges! It is great for you to encounter some difficult moments in your business, this will help you grow and know more. It was during COVID-19 that a lot of businesses scaled higher and increase in their sales.

The 2020 COVID-19 saga stormed a lot of businesses. While some were closing down, other businesses were scaling higher. During this time, a lot of business and religious centers maximized the use of social media to showcase what they were selling and offering. So many people were making massive sales, while others were shutting down. So, don't run away from your storm, don't run away from your business challenges. Embrace the hard times because they reproduce in you some strengths:

- ***Your emotional intelligence is improved.*** One primary key to make things work out successfully is your emotional intelligence. It is the ability to be aware of, express, and control your emotions. There are times when we give our 100% effort, but still, the goals we plan to achieve don't go come as expected. We fail and we may fail again. It is fine that we lose sometimes. See this as a normal part of any process.

What's important is how you learn from such loss, and utilize the lessons gained from those failures. When you can effectively handle your emotions in times like that, you can control the damage and become more efficient in all kinds of situations.

- ***New opportunities for creativity will open for you.*** Some of us were raised in this world with the belief of conforming to the rules of society. Because of that, our mindset is given to limited capabilities. Instead of thinking about how to be creative, we then begin to live with limited skills and dreams. When we have a never-give-up attitude, we start to see our life's real worth and dare ourselves to do unlimited things. We explore our talents and showcase our capabilities to create better things for ourselves and the whole society. We begin discovering the importance of creativity, and how being creative helps to find better opportunities and fresh perspectives in life.

- ***You will eliminate your fears.*** Significant things such as job promotion, graduation, a new house, relationships, and overcoming pains are defining moments of your perseverance and efforts. They are the results of your choice to continue reaching for the goals instead of stopping and giving up. A never-give-up attitude can be used to abolish doubts and negative thinking to make you stronger in facing everything.

Your success was the sweetest when you realized what you came through and what tough times had you defeat before you reach those goals. It's all about the attitude that aids in commencing a battle. It's about the way you continue that battle with the faith of winning in life.

- ***You learn something new.*** We learn a lot when we keep going. We can learn that there are hidden strengths and potentials within us. We learn how to keep ourselves motivated. More importantly, we learn not to give up, and also how we can effectively convert our failures to success. We become an inspiration to others, capable of doing greater things in the future.

- ***You will believe that anything you can perceive is possible.*** What is good in believing that anything is possible is that you will have the energy to power yourself up to take action. When you know that you are capable, you will overcome the things that may hinder your efforts. Often, the measure of success is between your perception and getting out of your comfort zone. It's your will to take actions. Of course, the only answer to that is to never give up.

## Success is Always Around the Corner

Hard work, they say, pays off eventually. Technically, there is no recognized basis to measure hard work or prove that it breeds success. However, often times, one finds comfort in the belief that each quality decision and effort invested into an idea is meant to produce the desired result - which is exactly what is needed to keep pushing. Although trials would come, nothing beats the strength of persevering in the face of these trials.

As a matter of fact, the hardest trials are the ones that come right before the breakthrough. Most times, it's hard to predict with clear precision what the end would be like from the beginning, but one might just be closer to achieving the desired goals than they even know it. Giving up takes that satisfaction of "knowing" away.

Think about names like Mark Zuckerberg, Steve Jobs etc., these are iconic people because their stories are sources of inspiration to millions of people around the world. For instance, the story of how Mark Zuckerberg dropped out of school to pursue a career in entrepreneurship is very popular on the internet. Despite having to make that hard decision at a stage in his life, it didn't stop the Facebook founder from forging ahead and building a company that is worth billions of dollars. As an entrepreneur, your hard work and dedication could be the spark that is needed to light the dreams of those around you and even spur them to greatness.

There's arguably something quite refreshing about knowing your story is a source of inspiration to others, but there is never an option for those who call it quits.

Every aspiring entrepreneur has to have at the back of their mind that the road to entrepreneurship is often patchy and rocky, but with determination they can actually achieve their ambitions.

## How to Motivate Yourself When You Feel Like Giving Up

We have all been at this point where we had big business ideas and dreams, but for whatever reason, we gave up along the way. Maybe you decided that the pain just wasn't worth it anymore and that it would take too much time, effort, and sacrifices to succeed. Maybe the journey took so long that you lost sight of why you started in the first place and eventually quit because you stopped caring about your goal. Or maybe you just hustled so long without seeing any results that you lost the belief in yourself.

Whatever it is, I have also been at that point where I felt like giving up. The fact remains that it is easy to quit when we lose sight of why we started in the first place. When you start dreading every day because you don't see yourself getting closer to your goals, it is important to find your passion and motivation again to keep going. After all, every business goal or even personal goal worth achieving requires some efforts and sacrifices. You can't expect to run a marathon without any pain. There will always be setbacks, oftentimes way more than you anticipated, but you can't let that stop you from living your business dreams! Every successful business owner had to go through some struggle to get to where they are now.

Most people think pain is bad. They think that the easier it is, the better. But actually, quite the opposite is true! The harder it is, the better! Think about this: have you ever grown from an easy task? I bet not! We only grow in the storm, our businesses also thrive in the middle of the wind - when it's tough, and we have to give it our very best. When you go to the gym to build your muscles, would you just lift easy weights a hundred times? No way! The only way to grow your muscles is by putting high weights (stress) on them. So, just as you grow your muscles by putting on some weights, you will also grow your business by going through some rigorous times and challenges.

When it gets tough and anyone else would understand if you quit, that's when you have to keep going! When everyone else is giving up, it's your chance to separate yourself from the masses, from the people that just kind of want it and aren't prepared to do whatever it takes. Adversity is your best friend if you learn to use it!

We all get stuck sometimes, but the question is, how do we get out of it? How do we keep going when the odds seem to be stacked against? Over the years, I have found several techniques that have been very useful to me whenever I was going through tough times. I will share some of them with you. These are like proven strategies or in other words, they are motivations that will help you to stand tall even in the midst of your difficult moments as a business owner.

- ***Embrace the struggle for it makes you stronger:*** As I have mentioned before, there is nothing worth having in life that comes easy. You will have to go through a lot of pains, sacrifices, and struggles if you want to live a great life; your business will have to go through some hurdles before it will be successful. While most people see this as a big problem and challenge, you must decide to embrace the pain because it will make you stronger! By fighting when everyone else would long give up, you not only strengthen your mental muscles, but also separate yourself from the set of people that don't want it as bad as you do.

Great businesses don't "emerge" in one night, they work thoroughly to get to the place they are. If greatness was easy, everybody would have been running marathons and enjoying their lives on a yacht right now. But, living your greatness is hard, and that makes it so great. Not everyone can do it, not everyone will be great; not every business will survive, thrive, and succeed, but as you are reading this book, determine and make up your mind to make something great out of your business. So, this is your chance to shine! Though it's hard at times, try to embrace adversity when it comes and use it as an opportunity to grow your business even more!

- ***Remember your "WHY"*:** Whenever you are struggling and it all seem to be overwhelming, it will be easy to forget why you started in the first place. Some challenges will not take it easy on business owners, but then, that shouldn't stop you from pushing. Whenever you feel like giving up, just remember why you started your business in the first place. Remember you want to take care of you family, you want your family to be proud of you, you want to make more money, go on vacations, buy a luxurious home for yourself, remember you want to make an impact, and also be financially independent. Just remember your "Why".

Ask yourself, why do I want this? Why do I have to earn in 6-figures? Why do I have to improve my relationships? Whether it is to prove your greatness to the world or make it a better place, find your reason to keep going even when all hell is breaking loose.

You can imagine if Bill Gates had given up years ago, then we would not have anything to call Microsoft today. It is important to know why you are doing the business you are doing and never give up until you succeed! If you can keep your eye and mind on your "Why", believe me, the drive and energy to do more will come upon you and help you push forward. Your challenges should not even stop you from trying. Stop focusing on those storms howling at your business, or your days are numbered. Keep your eyes on getting back to your fighting weight, on the positive effect money will have on you, the fact that you want to make your family proud, the good life you want to live, and so on.

- ***Think of the people you can't let down:*** Whatever you are trying to accomplish in life, there will be people who depend on you, support, or believe in you. Greatness isn't only about you, it affects everyone around you. It is not a selfish act when you live your greatness, it is in fact one of the most selfless things you can do, and more than success and monetary gains. Both are great if used them for a greater cause, but greatness also includes more than that. It is about making this world a better place. It's about living up to your full potential and giving the world your unique talents so that others may be inspired to do the same. It's about lifting people up and always looking for ways to grow and become better. With that in mind, do you think that the food you eat or the amount of time you spend gossiping and checking the news has effect on the people you love? Of course, it does! You need energy to be there for your family every day and need to work hard to provide for them. If you don't do that, you are not just selling yourself short, but also failing the people closest to you.

Whenever I feel tired and want to quit, I think of my family and my wife to motivate myself. These are the people that I cannot fail, and so it hurts to even imagine admitting to them that I failed because I didn't try hard enough. Shall I let you in on something? As a business owner, it is okay to lose, as long as you give it your best shot. When you can look at yourself in the mirror and know that you did the best you could, you can be proud of yourself. No matter how often you fail, if you keep pushing and working hard, one day you will succeed! Maybe not immediately, but definitely!

So, whenever you think of quitting, think of the people that you cannot fail. Maybe it's your family, friends, your spouse, or even your kids. Imagine walking up to that person and telling them that you failed because you just "didn't feel like it anymore." Think of the pain that would cause you and then go right back to work! Your business will succeed, I believe!

# Chapter 8

# Brand Advertising

---

***There is no shortage of remarkable ideas, what's missing is the will to execute them***

---

-Seth Godin-

As an entrepreneur, if you want to be effective in reaching consumers and building customer loyalty, you must consider various elements of branding. Certain elements draw consumers to the brand and can influence their choices. I will discuss some of those elements at the later part of this chapter.

The concept of branding may go as far back as 2000 B.C. when merchants began considering how they could sell their wares more effectively. Merchants in ancient Babylon developed sales pitches to lure in customers. Craftsmen branded or carved symbols on their merchandise to indicate their origin. Tavern owners hung attractive signs outside. The word "branding" for product marketing might have come into use in the 19th century when Western cattle ranchers started using hot irons to mark their livestock with the ranch's initials or a symbol. Their initial purpose was less marketing than protection from cattle rustlers, but the association stuck. Branding as mass marketing took off in the 19th century, as sellers of products like flour began thinking about ways to distinguish themselves from their competitors.

Branding is a strategy of creating a unique name, logo, image of a product to grasp the attention of customers. It helps the customers to distinguish a product from other sellers' products, establish fondness, and build trust. It does not only leave an impression in customers' minds but also allows them to know what to expect from the brand. It is one of the marketing tools used by a company to spread awareness about the product to the customers.

When a business or a company seeks to define its public image, it first must determine its brand identity or how it wants to be viewed by the public. Your goal as a business owner is to make sure that your brand is memorable and appealing to the consumer, or rather to the customers that the business is targeting, whether it is the singles, couples with small children, or affluent retirees, and so on.

A successful brand accurately portrays the message or feeling the company wants to get across. This results in brand awareness or the recognition of the brand's existence and what it offers. Once a brand has created positive sentiment among its target audience, the firm is said to have built brand equity. Some firms with brand equity and very recognizable product brands include Dangote, Coca-Cola, Ferrari, Apple, and Nike. If done right, branding results in an increase in sales, not just for a specific product, but for other products sold by the same company. A good brand engenders trust, and after having a good experience with one product, the consumer is more likely to try another product related to the same brand.

Creating a brand provides numerous benefits to a business. A business that gets its message across is able to induce and evoke emotion within its customer base. Consumers develop unique relationships with the business. The business in turn relies on these customers to help draw in others. Branding helps companies build trust and credibility that give them a competitive edge against other competitors. It also helps companies introduce new products and services. Consumers stay loyal to brands they know and trust and with whom they already have a relationship. That makes them more likely to spend when new products are released, even if they're more expensive. If you are familiar with Apple, I'll use them as a classic example. The company built a huge loyal customer base that is willing to overlook the higher price tag associated with an iMac, MacBook, iPad, or iPhone because of their loyalty to the brand. Its customers don't hesitate to replace their existing Apple gadgets with new ones as the company releases them.

If you're a business owner, whether small or big, you must thoroughly work on your branding. This will help the identity of your business or company. And when branding your business, make sure you think about something simple but unique. Don't start looking for an ambiguous business name and/or logo, rather consider what will be easy for people to pronounce, and identify.

## Brand Advertising

The goal of brand advertising is to foster long term positive recognition by establishing brand identity, credibility, loyalty, and connecting with prospects intellectually and emotionally. Its primary aim is to get people to believe in something. Hence, it is a strategy used by organizations to build customer loyalty and increase their base. Brand advertising also creates an immediate and favorable response to specific products or companies, which may be accomplished through jingles and images.

Brand advertising is used to establish awareness for a brand, a product, or a service in order to strengthen identity and increase customers' loyalty. It can employ all common advertising techniques, like social media advertising or search engine advertising.

It is a long-term measure and its results are not immediate. As opposed to performance-based advertising, brand advertising does not contain any direct call to action and therefore does not generate direct outcomes; its main goal is creating a lasting emotional connection to the brand, product, or service.

As a business owner, one powerful way by which you can gain access to people's hearts is through social media. Though social media today has done more harm than good to people which many can't even recover from, however, as a business owner, you need to deploy its use to your advantage.

You must see the good side of social media rather than noticing the negative impacts. So many businesses are generating millions of dollars simply because they are using social media tools to advertise their products, services, and brands. Some businesses have gone from low-income generating businesses to high-income generating businesses because they employ the use of social media to run advertisements for their businesses. Don't shy away from the good social media will do for your business, hence there is a need for you to embrace it to foster the viability of your business. The world has gone digital; people now transact business online. If an order for food can be placed via social media, then there is no business one cannot do or transact via social media. So many won't be able to walk down to your physical store, but they can browse through your store at the convenience of their home.

One of the reasons some businesses run down today is simply because their online customer base is so poor. To be a successful business owner, you must be able to build strong online customer relations. Don't focus only on those who are patronizing your physical store, you need to also focus on those who will interact with your business online. All I'm saying is, do not only build your brand physically, build it online also. Go digital. One mistake people make is that they think their kind of business cannot thrive in the online world. That's a big lie. Whatever business is, it will thrive on social media.  If you can have people who will patronize your brand in your physical store, there will definitely be people who will patronize you via your online store.

**Elements of Brand Identity**

Regardless of which business you do, chances are that competition is fierce. Countless businesses are established every year all over the globe; granted, not all of them will succeed, but some will. The question now is how do you set your business apart from the rest? The answer may not surprise you, it's "branding". The importance of branding can't be understated in the context of a global market with intense competition.

Branding requires you to truly understand the message you want your business to convey to the world, and to understand your customers and what you want them to take away from your business. One of the key parts of branding is establishing brand elements, and briefly, I will discuss what branding elements are. I will also give examples that you can use for your business survival.

Brand elements are the unique aspects of your brand, like name, logo, color schemes, etc. that create a cohesive, recognizable image for your business and extend into everything you create. Brand elements also help you stand out from your competitors. They are essential to business success and cannot be understated. I will discuss each type below.

- ***Brand name:*** A brand name is the words you use to identify your business/company and what you offer to the public, distinguishing you from other businesses and your competitors. Coming up with a brand name may seem easy, but it can have huge impact on the success of your business. For instance, if you need to build a new house, you may say or consider that you need a Dangote cement for the construction. The word "Dangote" is actually the name of a brand, while the actual product is the cement, hence "Dangote Cement".

- ***Logo:*** Your business logo is vital to your branding as it is one of the most recognizable aspects of your brand. Audiences will recognize you if it is out and about, on your emails, website, and maybe the physical products you sell. Logos, being the first thing consumers recognize about an organization, are an important detail to image. Often, a logo is used on everything the company or organization produces. It must speak to the brand's identity;

hence, colors, fonts, and images used in a logo should be unique and recognizable.

- ***Graphics and Images:*** More or less like logos, graphics and images as elements for your brand must not be difficult to define as they encompass all of the other brand elements that make your business unique. For example, your logo is a graphic you may include in a marketing email.

  When you share images, the style you use to edit them should be consistent and cohesive on all platforms and materials. For example, use the same filters over your images, crop your photos in the same way to be consistent.

- ***Slogans:*** Slogans are unique brand elements that don't necessarily apply to every single business, but, if used, they make up an important part of your branding. They can be used in marketing materials and included in commercials. Many slogans and jingles get stuck in consumers' heads, helping you retain the top in the mind of consumers. A slogan is how the company conveys its particular product to consumers. For instance, if you hear "Everywhere you go", the next thing that comes to mind is MTN. Likewise, if you hear or see the slogan "Just do it", you can immediately recall and identify that they're referring to Nike. Slogans or taglines are used to identify or state the uniqueness of a business, they add context to a logo by telling the consumer what an organization does and what to expect.

## Why are Branding Elements Important?

Now, you we can understand that branding elements allow businesses to choose how they want to be perceived in the potential customer's mind. Let's illustrate this with an example. If you saw a company that is dealing with robotics and futuristic technology, and their branding involved a font from a 1950s newspaper and had words like “vintage” and “classic” in their message, you would rightfully feel a disconnect between the company’s purpose and their branding. This is an extreme example, but it illustrates how important the choice and cohesion of branding elements are. It also shows how counterproductive a poorly chosen branding strategy could be.

Successful branding tells us a whole story about a company and their product. A well-developed branding strategy will tell you the purpose of the brand, how it sees its products, who they are appealing to, what goals they have, and what their core values are.

It is important to let your potential customers know all this information because it will help them choose which company, they want to do business with. By setting the right expectations for the customer and then delivering on them, you can guarantee that your brand experience is memorable. This is why understanding branding elements is so important. This is often what will separate a successful business owner from an unsuccessful one. Because branding elements aren't just about being flashy and loud, they are about conveying the right message in the right way.

The potential is virtually limitless. As you might know from your own experience as a customer, some companies have developed such successful branding strategies that their brands have become a part of popular culture. Think of terms as "googling" or the fact that just by saying "Just do it", "Everywhere you go", business brands will probably pop into your mind. These are all examples of extremely successful branding elements which help illustrate the brands' unparalleled potential and importance.

If you will see your business succeed and thrive, you must also build a sustainable business brand for yourself. Build it to the extent that whenever they see or hear about your company or business somewhere, something must definitely pop into their minds. In the 21st century, doing business is now more of strategy than what the tradition used to portray in the 19th century.

The secret to building a successful business is not far-fetched if only you would stick to what will make your business a thriving one.

## Chapter 9

# Making a Difference in Your Business

*Far and away the best prize that life offers is the chance to work hard at work worth doing*

-Theodore Roosevelt-

Having heard "Do your best to be the best", "Dare to be different", and other many times, these motivational lines also apply to business. If you must bring the best out of your business, you must be willing to go the extra mile. There is no common man who will ever finish the race with a common attitude. Show me an uncommon man and I will show you a man who will show forth an uncommon result to the world. Bringing something uncommon from inside of you requires that you put serious energy and effort into what you are doing.

This will start from recognizing the uniqueness and distinctiveness of your business. In the previous chapter, we discussed branding and the various branding tools you can use for the growth of your business. The success of your business lies in the amount of energy you can mount on yourself.

Every business has the capacity to make a difference, but not all will make a difference. All business owners need to know that the success of their business lies on their shoulders, not their workers. A business owner should rather be a person who has a great vision, passion, and a mind for expansion. Without any of these, no business owner will ever make any difference.

Ask yourself these questions: what are other businesses doing that I've not been doing? Can I do better them? How do I serve my customers better? How can I get my skills upgraded? Your sincere answers to these questions can help you build a more successful business.

Being different from the crowd in business will make you conspicuous. When your business is different, you attract attention and consumers begin to discuss your products and services. When more people discuss you, your business will come to limelight, triggering a desire among people to be part of the game. To be different is not an exciting science but it can be accomplished if you have the flair for innovating more often than the competition outside. This is because uniqueness is short-lived and someone is there always around the block to replicate it.

**Influencing and Focusing on Your Customers**

If your business will ever make a big difference, you should know by now that customers are the heart of every business. Without them, business cannot survive! No business ever patronizes itself, this is why you must focus on your existing customers. If you can successfully focus on your customers, then you're also building a successful customer base, and it is a successful customer base that will ensure or make a successful business.

Many business owners don't understand what it means to influence people; many aren't going into business because they also lack the knowledge. To influence people means to know and understand their basic needs, to heavily invest in what they need, and to give them the right treatment. Influencing others is essential, but it's more than just giving commands. Successful businesses are customer-focused, understanding the needs of their current customers.

If you know how to treat customers right, your business will be highly successful, because satisfied customers can drive profits through repeat business and referrals.

For as long as humans have been around, we've been asking ourselves questions about our purpose in life and how we can best fulfill it. These existential questions seem to be a part of human nature and often drive people to start social innovation projects so they can leave a meaningful mark on the world. But sometimes, it's hard to see what difference one person can make and how we can help our local and global communities. Even if you're not trying to solve world hunger or global warming, brainstorming ways to help your community can make a big difference.

When we help others, it doesn't stop with us. Studies have found that when we help others, those around us are more likely to help, too. This means that the more we give our time or resources to the issues we care about, the more others will give in return. In that way, one person's actions really can change the world for good.

Influencing and focusing on your customers depends on the business owner, you need to know exactly what your community needs and how you can meet that need. If your business will succeed, then you must also be diligent in making sure that your business is making efforts to know what it can do better to serve both the customers and the community at large. In this way, the business is making a difference, and success is inevitable.

## Can We Make a Difference?

Profit, profit, profit. That's the focus of every business, right? Well, that's true. Profit is important, in fact, for a sustainable business, but it doesn't have to be your primary focus. When you make a difference in your business, you profit. It is uniqueness that births value and value will give birth to profit; which means if you are not making a difference, then you probably might not make a profit. So, let it just be known unto you that if you cannot make a difference, you cannot make a profit.

Businesses that consciously focus on making a positive impact make 12-14 times more income than those who just focus on financial profit. Does generating that kind of revenue sound appealing to you? If yes, start making your difference henceforth. It isn't just for non-profits or social enterprises any more, making a difference is important to every works of life, because if you must excel, you must think of ways to do that even as a business owner.

You could even say that the purpose of business is to make a difference! Why did you start your business? You wanted to offer something that would be valuable to other people, right? Then, it means as you are doing your business you have decided to sign up for a total life or world of big differences. We cannot get through one day without making a difference. The question is, what kind of a difference do you want to make? We now have scientific proof that, the more you care about the happiness and well-being of your fellow humans, the happier you get. One pleasant side effect of making that kind of a difference is that, by changing the world around you, you also change yourself, and vice-versa. It is a virtuous circle.

## Making Your Business Unique from that of Your Competitors

Have you ever struggled to differentiate your business from that of your competitors? If so, you're certainly not alone. It is like that in every sector, where there are multiple businesses providing the same or very similar services, to the same group of customers. Any marketing message a prospect hears from you, they are likely to have heard in very similar terms from a competitor and most company Unique Selling Points are, in reality, far from unique. You need to know the business that stands out and demonstrates why they should be chosen over their competitors has the best chance of being successful. So, how can you avoid getting caught up in the mainstream and really stand out? This is where and why you need to be smart. You need to find unique ways of doing things, selling your product, and offering your services.

If your business must be unique and be different from that of your competitors, then you must treat your customers like royalty, even if you are not in the service industry. The belief that customer service only matters in the service industry is a myth. All customers have an expectation of great service and will not put up with waiting in long lines or receiving poor responses from representatives. Around 80% of customers state that they consider customer service a true test of a company's competence. Small businesses can do a whole lot better in the area of providing services as they have discovered the loyalty-generating power of remarkable customer support.

Then, you also need to consider the following:

- ***Solving your customer's problems:*** To make a difference in your business, you must be willing to be a problem solver. Every business uniqueness and even individual will gravitate towards solving some specific problems. People turn to a product or service because it solves a particular problem. Know what these issues are and tailor your services and the core marketing message that surround it to address them in the most efficient and cost-effective way. Play to your strengths. Be honest about your skill set and what qualifies you to address these pain points in a better way than your competitors.

- ***Be better at marketing***: As a business owner, if you cannot market yourself, then there is no point in finding yourself in the business world. Knowing how to market your product to your customers is one of those ways to upgrade your business financial status or profit.

Invariably, if you don't know how to market your services or products, your business will run at a loss. For all their similarities, most businesses genuinely do have unique points that set them apart, they just aren't very good at talking about them. Your marketing strategy shouldn't emphasize the ways in which you're similar to your competitors, but the ways in which you are different.

Don't be afraid to break the mold with your marketing communications. So long as you understand your ideal customers and what they are looking for, be bold, be out there, be innovative, be radical, and be strategic with your marketing. Work with an agency who knows what they're doing, and approach marketing in a consistent and measurable way.

- ***Have a genuinely unique selling point:*** Start by thinking of a genuinely unique selling point to offer your customers. Do this by looking at your skills and background, and determine how this adds value to your service in a way that can't be claimed by your competitors. For instance, as a business owner, you are different from most of your competitors by having a background in business coaching, rather than only the technicalities of offering your services or selling your products.

- ***Do business differently:*** As a business owner, you should be willing to learn from others. Look at the way your competitors do business, look at their sales process, examine how they treat their customers, how they deliver their service, and identify where there is room for improvement. These gaps are opportunities for you to differentiate yourself and to provide better customer service.

**Making a Difference Attracts Customers**

Any good thing will attract good people, expensive and well-packaged product will also attract expensive and well-packaged customers. More than ever before, consumers are now prioritizing socially-conscious brands and services. Millennials, that is, the 20th century generation, who represent a huge portion of consumers are leading the charge in this shift. They are much driven and attracted to products that speak to their mind rather than to their eyes. This is why most businesses are pumping their money into social media adverts and marketing. Studies have shown that modern consumers, especially millennials, will choose a brand that aligns with their values, supports a social cause, or practices good ethics over one that offers the cheapest prices. People want to feel good about where they're spending their hard-earned money, especially now, with the cost of housing and goods skyrocketing.

For you, this means that making a difference isn't just good for the world and your community, it's also good for your bottom line.

## How to Make a Difference

By now it's clear that making a difference is rewarding both internally and externally. Working for the greater good not only gives fulfilment to you and your team, but also attracts consumers to your brand. So, how can you make a difference?

There are many ways to create a socially-conscious or community-driven business. Below are some of the best ways.

- ***Supporting employees.*** Treat your workers well, give them the best treatment you could ever imagine, because the success of your business will lie solely on how you treat your employees. If you treat them poorly, your workers won't treat your business well. You can support your employees with health care benefits, on job training, and others as you may consider.

  If you want the best out of your business, listen to employee feedback. As a business owner, you should also create flexible work solutions and add new caregiving benefits as well as mental health resources to help employees balance competing demands of work and family.

- ***Expand your knowledge.*** There is always room to learn and improve. If you think your business has not reached its peak potential, take some time to speak to your employees, consumers, and the surrounding community about the impact your business has, probably positive or negative. Then you can formulate a plan on how to address these impacts.

In addition, it is important to upgrade your skills. Things keep evolving almost every year - what you know today can be obsolete if further study or upgrading is not made.

You must dare to sharpen your skills and professionalism every time; don't think you know it all, learn more and expand your intellectual horizon. If this will take you back to school for upgrade courses in specific areas of your business and skill, please do. This will ensure that you are well-informed and will portray you as qualified in your area of professionalism. Don't also neglect business seminars, learn from other professionals in your field, and connect with those who know better. Also, don't forsake the gathering of other successful business owners.

- ***Giving back to the community:*** Regardless of your business size, you can always give something back to your locality. This can make current and potential customers spot a difference in you. You may not have it all, but you can give your little money to support those within your local community.

  For any business scale, there are many ways to give back. For instance, you can decide to distribute free books to primary school pupils in your community, fill up potholes on the road that leads to the location of your business, or fix the street lights. These, among many others, can boost the reputation of your business and protect its interest.

You don't need much before you can give back.

Meanwhile, giving back to your community does not only have to do with doing something worthwhile for your external communities, you can also do for your immediate community, i.e. your employees. You can decide to give them little incentive just to compensate them for what they are contributing towards the success of your business. Lastly, your business can endeavor to give out to charity, NGO, and so on. Doing this can make others refer lots of potential customers to patronize you.

- ***Ensuring customer satisfaction:*** As a business owner who wants to make a big difference in your business, you must make the best product/service available to your customers. Making and offering an excellent product or service with a high value proposition helps give you a competitive advantage. And, besides the value proposition of a particular product or service that makes the business loved, it's often great customer service and knowing how to improve it that keeps customers returning. Happy customers often become repeat buyers, spreading your good deeds, quality products, and satisfying customer services to their friends, colleagues, neighbors, and so on.

By reading business books, studying your respective industry and competitors, and listening to entrepreneur podcasts by industry experts and successful entrepreneurs, you can gain valuable insights into bettering your offerings and finding business success.

- ***Do something totally new today:*** Sometimes, a new idea completely changes how people do things. Now, ask yourself: What new thing can I do to make a difference in my business today? Whatever comes to your mind in the course of answering, go ahead and do it. Don't wait till tomorrow before making the best out of your business. Don't be afraid to try something new. If you become a success, it's to your gain, and if it doesn't come out well, it's still to your advantage. Always know that if you don't try new things, you can't achieve great things.

Chapter 10

# Basic Principles for Business Success

---

***Successful entrepreneurs are lifelong learner who are constantly looking for ways to improve and grow***

---

-John D. Rockefeller-

Principles are kinds of rules, beliefs, or ideas that guide you. We can literally say that if a person has a good character, kind and ethical, then he has a lot of good principles. In general, a principle is some kind of basic truths that help you with your life.

A politician who tries to do the right thing rather than win votes is acting on principle. A person who has principles is a good, decent person. Likewise, if a person achieves great success in his lifetime, we will conclude that he knows the principles of success, hence his being successful. On the other hand, if you say someone has no principles, it means they're dishonest, corrupt, or evil.

"Work hard" is the mantra for success that is given to budding entrepreneurs, but in the 21st century, no single rule can be applied to it. You might even have heard people saying, "Don't simply work hard alone, you should work smart too." There are endless motivational and inspirational videos of successful businesses and of people who can go on and on with their advice. The thing is that success has different meanings for different people and even takes different paths depending upon its pursuer. It doesn't come easy, but at some point, you might even get what you want. But, remember, sustaining it is more important than attaining it.

Most businesses in the modern era fail because success gets in the head of the stakeholders and they eventually lose their vision. Therefore, no matter what, you must not stray from your vision because it is what inspired you to get started in the first place and it will keep you on the path.

For any business trying to survive in the 21$^{st}$ century, things are a tad easier as we have technology by our side. While this is so, it has also made the competition cruel. So, to fight, survive, and thrive in this competitive era, one needs to have insights on how to get the best out of the available resources, and of course, out of themselves. However, these things are certainly easier said than done.

Doing business in the modern era is a mix and match of several tips and tricks. It requires more than just a great idea or a product that people want to buy. To truly succeed, business owners must follow certain principles and guidelines that are proven to work. These principles are the foundation of any thriving business, enterprise, and company, and they can help business owners navigate the complexities of the modern business landscape.

The principles of any business success are the foundational pillars that guide entrepreneurs, managers, and business owners on their path to growth, profitability, and achievement. They encompass a wide range of strategies, values, and practices which when implemented effectively, can contribute to the long-term success and sustainability of a business. Businesses fail on a daily basis because most of them could not adhere to basic success principles, and if you as a business owner refuses to also consider these principles, failure and downfall will be inevitable. For instance, it is a principle when they advise on excellent service to clients.

If you then do not provide excellent services to your clients, you are joking with failure, because you are beginning to tamper with success principles. Everything, even life itself, has principles at which it operates with, which if you do not respect, you may lose your identity and be nowhere to be found at the later end. Business success also depends on many factors including having the right product or service, effective marketing, a good reputation, and financial stability. Businesses have to always put the customer first.

As stated in the previous chapter, any business has the capacity to be great and successful, but it is unfortunate that very few businesses will ever be successful, because so many entrepreneurs cannot pay the price of success.

I will be sharing with you some of the principles that will make you a success as far as your business is concerned. If you will work with them, your business will take a new shape; you will begin to record great success in months to come.

So, what are these principles? They are:

***The Principle of Effective Leadership***

If you don't understand the key to leadership, leading a successful business will remain a dream. Every successful entrepreneur is a great leader. Show me a successful business and I will tell you that there is a leader working from behind the scenes. As a business owner, you should develop the capacity to lead your team right, to execute and act on set goals. Many entrepreneurs lose their business due to the nonchalant attitude they posed towards their business.

Strong leadership is essential for business success. Effective leaders inspire and motivate employees, promote a positive work culture, and create an environment conducive to productivity and growth. They provide strategic direction, make informed decisions, and cultivate a cohesive team that shares the company's vision. Leaders achieve their goals by delegating responsibilities among the team. They tactically distribute work among subordinates and organize available resources required to reach the goal. Meanwhile, they also motivate people. They concentrate on the personal development of their team, besides working towards achieving organizational goals. They envision their business future growth and work towards achieving that.

Your business needs the right team of people behind it to attain success. However, this is only possible when things are right at the top. Put simply, you have to set a great example by becoming a great leader. If your leadership skills aren't there, the negative impact will filter down throughout the company. Evidently, it will limit your success and profits. Of course, hiring the right people will play a vital role in building the right team, and there is no question that your ability to lead by example and keep the staff motivated is one of the most important tasks that you'll ever face.

***The Principle of Vision Statement***

A vision statement is an aspirational statement made by a company that outlines long-term goals. An inspiring vision statement motivates both the employees and customers to be invested in their company's journey toward achieving its desired plans. And, inspired employees inspire customers, who can then inspire even more customers, helping to make the business's vision a reality. Bottom line? Your vision statement is important when starting a business.  It's typically ambitious and communicates how the company plans to make a difference in the world.

Think of it as a roadmap for making decisions that align with your company's philosophy and objectives. A vision statement is usually paired with a mission statement to guide planning. It doesn't have a set length. You can craft a one-sentence statement or write a three-page document discussing the company's future.

The goal of a vision statement is to differentiate you from competitors and focus efforts on achieving your objectives. Your vision statement is unique to your company, but it's useful to see how popular brands express their future goals. A good vision statement helps you:

- Inspire your team and keep them focused.
- Connect with customers in niche markets.
- Make smarter decisions.
- Attract top talent.

### *Importance of Business Vision*

Many business owners, particularly inexperienced start-ups, run their business without a vision in mind. They focus on short-term profits and forget about the long-term goal - to build a business that prospers! Is there any wonder why 90% of start-ups fail? If you're fortunate enough to be profitable from the outset of your business launch, then great! But be careful, it might not last.

There will be highs and lows and it's important to take the good with the bad. Don't get carried away with your initial success, but by all means celebrate your first win. Develop a vision which isn't based upon a monetary value and work towards it; this is the key to long-term growth and success.

- ***They provide the foundations for which to build upon:*** The foundation of a business is often lost in the day-to-day running of it. Businesses are all too quick to forget about what they set out to achieve once they're up and running, and this can affect the path for which the business takes moving forward. A vision statement can help to ensure the core goals of the business are apparent, and the values it possesses are understood. These can then be referred back to in other to ensure all actions are in line with the long-term goals.

- ***They provide purpose and direction moving forward:*** Again, purpose and direction can be lost, or might not have been there in the first place. Every business gets started for a reason - whether it's to fill a gap in the market or to supersede an existing business - there is always a purpose. A vision statement serves as a reminder to this purpose and helps mold actions towards a particular direction - to achieve the vision.

To summarize, vision statements are vital for any organization. They serve as a motivational reminder - when short-term success isn't apparent, long-term success still is. With the right foundations, direction and culture, no vision is unattainable!

### *The Principle of Mission Statement*

While all businesses have the same goal, that is, to make a profit, each business has a different mission. One entrepreneur might want their business to enlighten and educate their customers, another might want to provide the most joyful customer experience possible. To keep a business on track with its mission, business owners will often write a mission statement that concisely states the company's purpose.

A mission statement clarifies an organization's purpose for existing, what it wants to accomplish, and its core values. A good mission statement is short, ranging from one to three sentences long to a few paragraphs, and distills the operating principles that guide the organization's actions.

While it's not mandatory to have one, many business owners find it helpful to write and keep a strong mission statement on hand to help steer the business when opportunities or challenges arise. Additionally, it can help employees understand company values and culture, as well as explain these to potential customers, board members, and investors.

Businesses often post their mission statement on their websites under "Mission" or fold it into the "Our Story" section, however, you can also choose to keep your mission statement within the confines of the company; each business owner can decide for themselves who the internal and external audience of their company's mission statement will be.

## Importance of Business Mission Statement

A mission statement is your reason for being. It captures what you do, who you do it for, and the benefit or impact. A mission statement is more than just words on a page, it's the beating heart of your company and the central pillar of your company's success. Without a good mission statement, your business lacks direction and motivation. Your team won't have a shared understanding of priorities and goals, and your target audience won't fully grasp why they should choose you over the competition.

But, crafting mission statements is harder than it seems. Your mission statement needs to be authentic, yet aspirational, broad, yet focused. If done right, it can guide business decisions, rally your team, enable economic growth, and attract ideal customers.

- ***Creating identity:*** Mission statements create the core identity of a company and establish a basis for everyone in the company to make decisions. They contribute to a company's brand and encourage unity among everyone who supports or works with the company. A company's identity differentiates it from competing organizations, and the mission statement is one of the most defined ways to express that identity to others.

- ***Developing purpose:*** A strong mission statement gives employees purpose and improves engagement in their work. It enables them to see the meaning and purpose of their work by giving them clear reasons why their job benefits a larger goal. Employees see the positive aspects of their daily activities, boosting morale and creating long-term employee investment in the workplace culture.

- ***Improving performance:*** Mission statements provide a clear goal for employees and can improve their job performance. They are a great way to motivate the staff to work towards a company's long-term plans for growth.

A good mission statement creates an environment that encourages everyone to produce high-quality work and hold high standards for themselves. Employees can engage with a company's core values by reading its mission statement and applying those ideas to their work.

## The Principle of Planning and Strategy

Another great business principle you need to take note of is planning. Planning is "thinking before the action takes place". It decides beforehand what, when, and how the task is to be accomplished. It is not exactly the same as strategy, which is nothing but "a comprehensive plan." The strategy is all about using a trick to gain success for a particular purpose. It is the skill of managing the affairs of the enterprise.

Planning is an organized process of thinking in advance about a future action. It means the preparation of the plan, i.e. the sequence of steps which will help in achieving organizational objectives. It is among the five management functions apart from organizing, controlling, motivating and leading, and decision-making.

A future-oriented activity that takes place in routine decisions of a family, a friend group, a college, government, and most importantly, in business management, it requires good judgment skills to choose which action is to be done earlier or later to avoid overlapping in actions.

Strategy is a master game plan designed to achieve the objectives of an organization. It is a mix of competitive moves and actions made by the top-level management for the accomplishment of goals successfully. They are dynamic and flexible in nature. Strategies are based on practical experiences, not on theoretical knowledge, i.e. they are realistic and action-oriented activities. It requires deep analysis of the managers on any move or action, implementation timing, the sequence of actions, outcome, competitors' reactions, etc.

In the business world, corporate strategies are made for the expansion and growth of entities, which include mergers, diversification, divestment, acquisition, and many others. Strategies are made according to the present situations and conditions prevalent in the business environment, but it can't be said that they are perfect because of the changing needs and demands of the people; strategies may fail.

Successful businesses develop comprehensive strategies and detailed plans. This involves conducting market research, analyzing competitors, identifying target audiences, and defining unique selling propositions. A well-crafted strategy allows businesses to adapt to market dynamics, seize opportunities, and mitigate risks. The major differences between planning and strategy are:

- Planning is anticipation and preparation in advance for uncertain future events. Strategy is the best plan chosen among the various alternatives for accomplishing objectives.

- Planning is like a map for guidance, while strategy is the path which takes you to your destination. Strategy leads to planning, and planning leads to programs.

- Planning is future-oriented, whereas strategy is action-oriented.

## The Principle of Marketing

Can you market your product? Can you advertise what you are selling? Well, in one of the past chapters, I have vastly explained the necessity of marketing to your business. The success of your business depends ultimately on how important and serious you take your marketing. Producing goods or services is one thing, but those efforts can be redundant if you can't convince people to buy or use them.

Without sales, you don't have a business, you simply have a very expensive hobby. Therefore, for your business to record a huge success, marketing has to be considered as one of the most important aspects of your entire operation.

Nowadays, the internet is one of the most powerful resources available. A well-designed website is your portal for generating sales from a worldwide audience. Meanwhile, a strong search engine ranking will improve your localized sales too; after all, most consumers use the internet to find businesses in the local area. And, mobile searches are quickly taking over desktop searches, so it is essential to maintain some kind of visibility online. One of the key tips in marketing is the ability to show the personality of your business as people buy into the company as well as the products. Social media is a strong asset in marketing your brand and forming relationships with your customers.

Meanwhile, there are four major principles of marketing today. These are like guide that will help you place a premium on your marketing. They are the 4 Ps of marketing. Though, these principles are more than four, I will just briefly discuss four now. They are product, price, place, and promotion.

- Product: The tangible item or service that you're selling. Now, you need to get it clear that before your business can make a good break, you need to know if it addresses the needs, wants, and expectations of your prospective customers. If you are marketing the wrong product or services to the wrong prospect, then you are in for a shock; you should be assured that your business won't get a good break. In doing business, you must be ready to give people or sell to them what they will buy, rather than selling to them what you think will sell.

- Price: It may take some trial and error, but it's important to get your pricing strategy right you're your price is too high, there is a high probability that you'll lose customers. However, it is imperative to know what the market price is saying about your business before placing your price.

- Place: To market your products and succeed, your business must be located in a viable place where people can easily access your market.

- Promotion. This is what most people think when they think of marketing. Promotion includes tactics for sales, advertising, events, and other marketing channels to get your offerings in front of your target market.

## The Principle of Consistency

Why is consistency so important? Imagine if you were training for a marathon, and one day you decided to stop running. You might be able to get away with that for a few days or even weeks at the beginning of your training, but eventually, it will catch up with you. It's the same when it comes to achieving success in life; consistency is key!

Consistency is the critical driver for success. Being consistent means dedicating yourself to your goals and staying focused on the things and activities to achieve them. It requires a long-term commitment from you and involves sustained effort in doing actions repeatedly until you achieve your goals. Discipline, accountability, and responsibility are all parts of staying consistent. Consistency can spell the difference between failure and success; it can help anybody to achieve success in any field of endeavor.

It can be pretty easy to see why many people cannot be successful in their lives nowadays because of the way our society works and the proliferation of technology everywhere. The world today revolves around providing instant gratification, and the presence of technology has made people more impatient, wanting quick results. With just too many distractions, people's minds have become muddled up about what they want to achieve in life; there's a lack of focus on what they want to do. Pair this all up with the lack of discipline, accountability, and responsibility, and it's easy to see why many people struggle with maintaining consistency.

## How to Practice Consistency for Personal Development

The power of consistency is integral to achieving success in whatever you wish to do in life. So, the first thing that you can do to maintain consistency is to have a clear goal in mind. Without a clear goal, it's hard to get motivated in anything that you do. If you're having difficulty having a goal in life, maybe you can take some inspiration from other people's experiences and stories. Try reading books or get a life coach who can help guide you in getting clarity and focus in your life. Your goals are what will serve as the driver for your motivation and consistency.

Once you have your goals, the next step is to create a plan to achieve them. Your overall goals are broad in vision and scope, so break them down into smaller bits that you can achieve in shorter periods. For example, if your dreams will take ten years to complete, plan in detail what you will have to do for every year and then focus on the first year: what you must do for every month, then weeks, and then days. By creating a schedule and timetable and doing all these breakdowns, you will see what you need to do precisely at specific points in time and everything becomes clear.

## Reasons Why Staying Consistent is a Key to Success

There are several reasons why consistent hard work and maintaining it can lead us to achieve tremendous success in life.

- ***Accountability:*** Performing actions consistently involves doing the same activities almost every day (we do need breaks sometimes). The moment we skip doing something for a day, or even two, and then our objective fails; it's easy to see why such a thing happened. Being consistent makes us accountable for all our actions. There is nobody else to blame if you are the one doing the activities needed to meet goals. We are missing out on a workday or two means we might need to adjust our actions and behaviors to complete plans.

- ***Trust:*** Practicing consistency in our everyday lives helps build our trustworthiness with other people. It's easy to preach to others, but it might be harder to do what we say. People who "walk the talk" look very credible and trustworthy in the eyes of other people. When others trust you, it makes you feel good about what you are doing, and you know that what you are doing is well worth it. Being trusted by others also helps build self-confidence and creates the momentum to push forward with meeting all of our goals and objectives.

- ***Relevance and reputation:*** Concerning trust, maintaining consistency in our actions can make us relevant and build our reputation to others, especially if you are in business or a leader in some endeavor. Consistent hard work leads to long-term results, and people would like to work with someone who has a proven track record of accomplishing things. In business, this can mean more opportunities for clients. Doing your work consistently and earning good results can make a big difference, either in getting a promotion or staying a rank-and-file employee in a company setting.

- ***Discipline and self-control:*** Being consistent can be challenging as it requires a lot of self-control, and it can be an entirely new habit if one is not used to being consistent in doing things. Practicing consistency instills discipline and makes us focus and more aware of what we have to do. It can be pretty tough to let go of old habits, but if we want to improve things and achieve personal growth, we have to be consistent in everything we do.

## The Principle of Creativity

Entrepreneurship and creativity go hand in hand. Unfortunately, creativity can easily be overshadowed and stifled by business processes, leaving it simmering on the back burner rather than being a driving force. The truth is, creativity actually helps every aspect of business, so it's something that needs to cultivated and maintained.

Creativity in business is an ability entrepreneurs possess that allows them to develop new and imaginative ideas regarding processes, products or materials. Businesses can use creativity in the workplace to create innovative solutions or more positive and collaborative work environments. The creative process also involves asking questions or looking at problems from diverse perspectives. These qualities can help promote more productive brainstorming and collaboration across teams.

Encouraging creativity in the workplace can help boost business success. Creative thinking allows individuals to develop new or innovative ideas and challenge norms or old ways of thinking. These behaviors can help businesses create products, services and other offerings that differentiate them from their competitors and address consumers' demands in new ways. It's important for companies to assess new situations quickly and develop strategies to navigate them to handle changing markets and consumer trends.

With creativity, businesses can meet existing challenges and think ahead. By implementing regular brainstorming or creative-thinking processes, people can continue to develop innovative ideas that meet their markets' current and future priorities and preferences.

## How to Foster a Creative Mindset in Your Business

Maintaining creativity while working in the business world can be a struggle. We occasionally have to cope with tedious tasks that don't call for original thought. Working with existing work practices and concepts makes sense, especially in mature businesses. At that point, some companies want to move away from experimentation and toward stability since they are unwilling to take any chances. Our creative side may never altogether leave us, but we can lose touch with it.

Therefore, we should be careful not to stifle our imagination and devise innovative ways to either better our performance, or propose ideas that could benefit the entire department or business where we work. When I started my business, I had a creative mindset, from design to strategy, etc., to bring the notion to reality.

- ***Remove limitations:*** Unbelievably, limiting our employees to a standard nine-to-five schedule can prevent them from completing their most satisfactory job. Offering flexible work schedules and home-based working options might help employees be more productive and creative.

- ***Act on good ideas:*** If they believe their suggestions will be used, employees are more likely to make them. Employees may stop sharing their requests if they feel they are not being taken seriously. When putting a fresh, original idea into practice, we must make it a point of duty to let the staff members know.

- ***Set the stage for brainstorming:*** Without the right setting and resources, we can't expect our staff to brainstorm efficiently. We should design a workplace that encourages innovation and creativity to position our company for success. One of the best ways to promote brainstorming is to give our staff a piece of paper to jot down their thoughts.

- ***Encourage individuality:*** It is essential to make it clear to our staff that we respect their opinions. It sounds easy, but staff members sometimes feel it's better to keep up with their workload, fit in, and avoid becoming a squeaky wheel since they get used to feeling like part of the pack.

## The Principle of Mentorship

A mentor is someone who has priceless experience that you don't have yet, who has made all the necessary mistakes on the road to success, learned from them, and is willing to pass on those lessons to you. The world of entrepreneurship is one filled with resources. From online publications to peers, friends and family, advice about starting and running a business abounds. But, a dedicated business mentor with experience in your field can make the most impact on the growth of your business.

A true mentorship relationship is a two-way street – your mentor gets to learn about new strategies from you while you gain wisdom from them. On top of that, it's a (usually) free resource to help you start and grow your small business. Business mentors are a must-have in any entrepreneur's toolbox, from the day-one business owner to the established CEO. Mentors are usually experts in their field, often bringing decades of niche, industry knowledge to their mentees.

The key win of building a mentorship relationship is the unique and specific instructions you'll receive. Far from the generic advice of online contents or the well-meaning family member, mentors' advice is grounded in real-life experiences. A small UPS survey of customers found that 88% of business owners who reported having a mentor found it invaluable. Mentors motivate you through actionable guidance and resources. For example, you may go to a mentor asking for help on your financial statements. A good one will not only provide their experiences but also may provide templates and a referral to an accountant for the next steps.

But mentors certainly gain from their interactions with mentees as well. Many guides eager entrepreneurs as a way to give back to their communities. Further, they may use the opportunity to instruct a younger business owner as a way to sharpen their teaching or consulting skills.

## Why Every Entrepreneur Needs a Business Mentor

A mentor doesn't just have a good grasp of the specific knowledge you need to succeed, like how to create better Facebook ads or how to bring a product to market, they also possess an intuition developed over the course of many years doing what you hope to do, and their knowledge can help you confirm, abandon, or shape some of your own business instincts. An experienced mentor helps you find your best self-faster than time alone would allow.

Mentorship occurs naturally in nearly every industry. But in the world of business, especially, you'd be hard-pressed to find a success story that didn't involve a trusted adviser along the way:

## Importance of a Business Mentor

As an entrepreneur, you wear many hats and are responsible for a lot of different moving parts in the business. From product development to marketing to sales, it can be difficult to keep everything intact. A business mentor can help you stay on track and provide insightful guidance when you need it. If you think otherwise, you're missing out.

- ***Mentors can assist in building your company's culture:*** Organizational culture has a key role in the success or failure of a business. A good culture keeps employees motivated and committed. Mentors can help you to develop a culture that supports the integrity of the organization.

- ***You receive reassurance and encouragement:*** Having a business mentor can make you feel less alone or isolated. You receive reassurance and encouragement from someone who has been in your shoes before, providing you a boost when your self-confidence takes a knock. Mentors will give you insights on how to take the next step with your business, with the experiences that will help you to remain positive, giving you constructive feedback on your ideas and advice that helps you succeed.

- ***You realize more opportunities to succeed:*** As I've discussed here, a business mentor has the potential to offer new ways of thinking and an outside perspective on your goals. They can provide you with valuable information and advice about your approach and your business. They can help by giving feedback to improve your weaknesses and build on your strengths, and help you to prioritize and remain focused on the big picture; you'll have someone to bounce your ideas off. Package all this, and you'll develop the sixth sense that will lead to the realization of more opportunities to succeed.

- ***You have someone to make you accountable:*** Having a mentor makes you more accountable. If you know that someone is going to hold you accountable for your actions and decisions, then you will be more likely to take those actions and decisions.

## Business Success FAQs

- ***How can I measure the success of my business?***

  Start by defining what success means to you and what takes your priority: Is it sales, growth, customer satisfaction, or brand recognition? Besides running a profitable business, do you value a collaborative and engaged workforce? Once assessed, you can measure your success through data collected via A/B testing, customer reviews, and email open rates, among other metrics.

- ***How long does it take to achieve business success?***

  Well, there is no set timeline for achieving business success. However, you can start by creating a business strategy to reach your goals. By mapping out the incremental steps to reach certain benchmarks from units sold to new hires, you can develop a general timeline to achieve success based on your experience and industry standards. Keep in mind, your timetable could change or take longer than estimated due to the ever-changing commerce landscape.

- ***Is there one formula to achieve success?***

More or less like asking about the principles that make businesses succeed. There's no single formula for success or every business will succeed. While owners of small businesses have different goals and priorities, there are some key markers that make a business successful. These include having an excellent business idea, vision and passion, and being a hard worker. If you are a leader with empathy and willing to delegate responsibilities to your team, you embody some of the traits required to achieve success.

## *ABOUT THE AUTHOR*

*Stephen Ayodele ISOLA* is a growth strategist, one of the global voices in this generation, an astute entrepreneur, a thoroughbred professional and a pastor. He bagged his first degree in Linguistics/Yoruba, after which he obtained PGD both in Missiology and Theology.

Being a passionate, resilient and an ardent lover of youths, Ayo Isola as fondly called represents a spectrum of Nigerian youths and particularly the Christian youths across all denominations as he strives to add unquantifiable value to the nation's economy and the church at large.

He is the lead pastor in RCCG His Glory Sanctuary Area, Ado Ekiti, Ekiti State.

Also, the Provincial Youth pastor, Ekiti province Four. His vision is to help many young people to fulfill their dreams and purpose in life.

Ayo Isola is the MD of Supreme Joy Global Resources Company Ltd, he also found AIHH FOUNDATION whose mission is to practically spread God's love. He is married to Dcns.

Deborah Ayo-Isola and they are blessed with wonderful Children.

## Others Books written by Ayo Isola

**YOU ARE POSSIBLE**

*By Ayo Isola*

**50 VIRTUES THAT WILL MAKE YOUR LIFE WORTHWHILE**

*By Ayo Isola*

www.ingramcontent.com/pod-product-compliance
Lightning Source LLC
LaVergne TN
LVHW041156150826
845673LV00001B/182

* 9 7 8 9 7 8 9 0 8 9 8 5 7 *